Creating your future

Destiny

Finding Your Way Home

By D Donovan

----

www.destinyretreats.com - Retreats and Meditations for the spirit

Copyright © 2008 D Donovan. *All rights reserved.*

ISBN: 978-0-578-01844-7

All rights reserved by the author. No part of this publication may be reproduced, stored in a retrieval system or transmitted in any form or by any means electronic, mechanical, photocopying, recording or otherwise, without the prior written permission of the author.

All of the participants portrayed herein are fictional composites of possible experiences you can have at a Destiny Retreat. None of the participants in this account are real. Any similarity to anyone who has attended a Destiny Retreat is a coincidence. Experiences at a Destiny Retreat are unique to every individual. Results will vary.

Therapists are always present at a Destiny Retreat and may alter activities to fit the needs of the group.

In Silence
Inside
I Found Home

To:
Mom & Grandpa for their love and guidance
Jerry for his love and protection
&
To David, Barbara, & Bryan, who inspire me to focus on a destiny of
Love, Peace and Compassion
&
A World of Peace.

To the Facilitators of Destiny:
Focusing on Love is
the only reality to create!
Thank you for supporting the reality of peace!

To my grandchildren, and all the children of the Universe, &
to the planet:
I dedicate my life to your peace, love, and compassion
&
abundance.

Remember the focus is love!

In Loving Memory of
David Donovan

TABLE OF CONTENTS

Acknowledgments iv

Introduction ix

1. Finding Your Way Home 20
2. Who Are You? 39
3. Silent Consciousness 45
4. Looking Yourself in the Eye 60
5. State Your Intention 73
6. Remember Love 81
7. Breathing Destiny 92
8. I Am the Element 141
9. I Made It Up 159
10. Integrating Love & Fear 188
11. God in the Oneness 228
12. Breathing Heart Dance 238
13. Being Peace 246

Introduction

God is thoroughly expressing my life destiny, this life purpose through me, in my complete awareness at all times now. I am one with God.

I have always been involved in helping others. It started out as a dynamic codependency. I looked around one day at the fact that I was always trying to fix or help everyone with my own egotistical energy, and asked God for a direction. With that request, I found an answer, and took the path to become a Marriage and Family Therapist, and an Alcohol and Drug Counselor.

Now, if you looked at codependency from a spiritual perspective, whatever I am actually doing for others, I am doing for myself. After all, we are all connected to one another no matter what illusions of aloneness we have woven around our existence. If it is true that all reality is one unified whole, and that the multiplicity of reality is an illusion, then being helpful makes perfect sense. The oneness of being, the tapestry that contains every experience, every element, every belief may seem too complex to comprehend, and yet even if we do not have lofty aspirations to contact the expanding Cosmos, we could still acknowledge that our part of the whole experience is meaningful and of unique contribution.

More simply, everything that you do affects me, and everything that I do affects you. Awakening to your personal energy output as well as to your energy needs (that is, finding out about where you put your personal energy in life) is one of the single most important lessons you can experience in this life. Energy flow determines your life. Observing, manipulating, and nurturing your personal energy, your creative ability, and your personal path in this life are transformational. All the while, remember that energy is boundless, infinitely available, and that what we give to others always returns to us because we are all one.

My friends' problems occupied huge portions of my time in my early twenties. I spent hours on the phone sympathizing with their problems. I tried and tried to fix everyone else's problems, including my husband (now ex), his sister (now deceased probably from her problems), and anyone else. You might say that I was a magnet for those with energy needs, and I was the free flowing energy supplier – very much like a drug supplier. I allowed my drug addict sister-in-law to live in my house so I could help fix her, and in doing so, fix her young children. As was to be expected, all of my fixing did not work since the energy was all mine! Oh sure, it may have temporarily helped in some cases, but for the most part, all I was accomplishing was, at best, to hold the problems at bay, barely treading water. In reality, I was giving energy to problems and therefore fueling their ongoing existence, becoming a lifeline. The so-called problems were in fact given additional life from my boundless sources of energy, which I was in fact tapped into because of deep spiritual practices. Enabling, the unflattering term for this life-consuming activity, is an apt description for the detrimental, controlling, and well-meaning help I so freely gave.

Like any good supplier of energy, eventually the output may expend the input, and the consumer is left without an adequate source. The consumer can find a new codependent, brimming with energy, expectation, and enabling, who is waiting to "help." With the failure of my fixing, and my own deep-seated self-esteem problems, I continued to never feel good enough, casually confirmed by the recipients of my dwindling energy. I suffered from severe depressive cycles all along, most of the time keeping my own problems at bay until they would erupt with a nasty flare of my own acting out, or anger, and then to die down again and be suppressed with high tolerance. After all, if I was good enough, so I thought, my help would help, I would never lose my patience, and I would be able to control myself. Sometimes, I was trying very hard to improve myself. Other times, I was in such a self-destructive depression and nervousness that it took control of my life. All the while, I gained weight, as I soothed my emotions with food, religion, and acting out sexually; a result of my own untreated childhood traumas.

I felt that I had to find an answer to all these problems of my life. I needed to become a better person and take everyone around me with me! My three children continually motivated me to move toward self-improvement, more for their future than my own. One of the best attributes, for a gem may be found in all flaws, is that all this motivation to save others still propels me to grow and learn about the world. My children are still the best teachers in my life, bringing lessons in love. Naturally, at first I thought that I was here to teach them! Turning my perspective around to look at the lessons that everyone is teaching me is how I arrived here today, writing this book.

Lucky for me, I was born with an on-going conversation with God. I do not remember a time when this conversation has not been with me. I always talk to God. I hope you know about those conversations when everything gets bleak and you have one of those, "Look, God," conversations. If you do not seek God when everything is going badly, what do you seek? It was through one of those "Look, God," discussions that God blessed me with a third child, who made it through a maze of scar tissue to become my third son, a master disguised as a child.

Profound insights, directions, and answers erratically appear, as I am able to listen and accept that I am more than just my mind and body. One of the most profound answers that I have ever received in one of those quiet mental times involved a retreat that was to be known as Destiny Retreats, which is the topic of this book. This profound offering that fell from the sky from somewhere outside my limited thinking is still taking place in Sedona, Arizona; or at other spectacular locations several times a year.

One day in 1996, while blowing my hair dry and consciously quieting my mind, the inspiration to write a script for a retreat blew in on the wind. The script is for Destiny, an advanced spiritual growth retreat for people who would like to find or focus on the meaning in their lives. Destiny Retreat is for seeking, finding, and practicing a life of meaning. Life contains many a paradox that you encounter at a Destiny Retreat. Finding your way home to your heartfelt connections is often a journey through complicated, multidimensional realties, which become an integration of all the facets you face in life, none more relevant than the other. With integration of the facets of your life, a profound enormity of meaning floods into your being.

The day I heard the wind speaking through the blow dryer began like any other day, with the hair dryer taming the wildness of long straggly hair. But along with my usual routine and usual nervous energy, I was over the top with anxiety about an upcoming personal growth seminar; Challenge is the seminar in which I would climb fifty-foot telephone poles and walk across wires strung into the nothingness of the thin air. Challenge is me facing a perceived near-death experience! In fact, in my mind, I was preparing to face death to go to this seminar. It was because of this anxious mind talk that I consciously dismissed my thoughts, silenced the pervasive near-death thoughts in my mind, and instead, heard whispering in the silence; the words that would become Destiny.

Within the silence, the words began to appear that day. It is

Introduction

so strange that when you silence your ordinary thoughts, something astounding can fly forward into being, a moment of pure creativity. Within silence, one can make contact with something higher than the ordinary mind, hear the answers to long sought after questions, and even more, become questionless.

Every day before work, the script for the retreat blew in with the wind. When I completed the rough draft, I tried to give the script to a friend of mine, the owner of the Challenging personal growth retreat company. At that time, I worked with her as a facilitator, on her request. Thanks to her, I learned to stand up to my fear of speaking and facilitating. She was reluctant about a retreat with so much silence and spirituality, at first. She changed her mind back and forth several times. She scheduled the retreat and then changed her mind again, canceling it.

One day, when we were sitting in a hot tub as she finally read over the script, she looked into the sky and said, "Look at the 'V' in the sky. There was a 'V' in the sky just like that one when I wrote my personal growth seminar. Destiny will be a success."

A year later, without anything ever happening with this retreat, she gave Destiny back to me, and said she had no problem with my doing it with my partner Cheryl, my son, David, and my husband, Jerry. At the time, we all worked with her either as facilitators or facilitators in training. I want to personally thank her for setting me free. I also want to thank her for the gift of *Finding Your Way Home*.

Within a few days, we took a trip to Sedona to look for a site. We scheduled a weekend trip to look at various sites in that area. Why go all the way to Sedona for Destiny, which by the way was aptly named by my Challenging friend's son? Sedona is known for its intense magnetic energy. This type of energy would be a great benefit to the process, and the red rock splendor is awe-inspiring! Sedona encourages insight, especially spiritual insight. Through a series of coincidences, we set out on a dirt road adventure to see the first site of the weekend. The place was an oasis in the sweltering summer desert. The staff invited us in and offered us healthy food, including some fabulous vegan brownies! The first site we visited hosted Destiny for several years before we began experimenting with other beautiful areas. This site encompassed red rock magnificence, star-studded skies, and red dusty trails up a vortex of energy where you can rediscover a shaman's cave carved by nature, still inspiring and nurturing the humans chanting on top of the world. It is a place of angels.

I could go on and on about the mystical discovery of our sites, but that is the stuff for another book. The book of our travels and coincidences will be coming out soon, and another one about creating a perfect relationship. The coincidences are too numerous to go into right now, but they are amazing. Suffice it to say that we have had one mysterious experience after another while working on Destiny, and our advanced retreats as well.

Cheryl and Jerry helped to polish the retreat contents. Jerry provided most of our inspirational music. He managed to call out the love in their hearts with beautiful music. David, one of my sons and teachers, is the co-author of one of our favorite meditations called *Remember Love*. David and I both wrote a meditation on the same day. Neither of us was aware that the other one was creating what would be mirror meditations of each other. It was my intention to use a meditation about destiny every day of the retreat, repeating it for emphasis. However, with the amazing coincidence of *Remember Love* and *Destiny* (the meditation) we have two very similar and yet different meditations for two days. Just as nothing I am saying will be new, the meditations are differently worded repetitions of the

Introduction

same profound message. These meditations and the others at the retreat are guides to expand your heart beyond the limitations of your mind, and then to begin the process of integration.

We not only offer Destiny Retreat, a four-day retreat in Sedona, but we also have Being Peace, a five-day advanced, shape-shifting retreat in the Four Corners region, and Angel Training, a five-day facilitator training held in various locations. We also have a meditation CD called *Finding Your Way Home*, (Cornelius & Donovan-Vaughn, 1996) which features the voice of Cheryl Cornelius, music by Rick Daugherty. This meditation is the first one you hear when you attend Destiny. Soon, all the guided meditations will be available!

This book is a guide for how to create your destiny. It follows the path that you would follow when you attend a Destiny retreat. Although it cannot ever give you the experience of being there, it will give you much of the knowledge. Nothing will quite compare to the experience of being in a group doing this retreat. In our virtual world, the computer programmers continually aim for ever more realistic programs. But no matter how many words or programs, the best way to achieve inner peace is through the actual experience and practice. You can read about it but you will not know it.

Spiritual experiences are difficult, almost impossible to verbalize (Hardgrave, 2003). Creating destiny is an eloquent spiritual experience, and as such, no words can possibly equal the glorious feeling of finding your way home. When you find your way home, inside, you will never again be alone. The creation of your destiny becomes a never-ending adventure into an expanding universe of possibilities

The book is written in the order in which the Destiny Retreat appeared those first few days from the wind. Since much of the Destiny Retreat is introspective and silent, the chapters provide additional explanations of the concepts of destiny – peace, love, and compassion. Instructions for the various techniques to practice in your daily life along with journal questions are included to aid in the expansion of your consciousness.

Beginning with Chapter One, Finding Your Way Home, you will begin your journey inside. Your personal music will play, echoing long forgotten emotions, and a mission that you carry in your very soul. You are looking at your life and beginning to release some of the many worn out defenses, beliefs, and goals that you are using to trudge through your daily life.

As you enter Chapter Two, you will define who you are, where you are in your life, and where you are going. You will look at your agreements in life!

In Chapter Three, you find out about silence, consciousness, and how to use a journal to change your mind, and guide it into creating the destiny you want in life. Silence is suggested as the best way to hear what your mind, emotions, and feelings are creating. How can you hear the voice of God when you are always talking over that still quiet voice emerging from within your heart?

Now, you are ready to look upon a world of mirrors in Chapter Four. In randomly encountering the people in your life, the coincidences are overlooked as nonessential surprises. This chapter explores the possibility that you are writing the script and calling forth the players, without every realizing your power.

Chapter Five reintroduces you to stating your intentions while restructuring your focus on realizing that maybe you don't know what will make you happy. Why are you on this planet?

In Chapter Six, you will be remembering love. Wouldn't a life without love be meaningless? This chapter explores the remembrance of love that goes beyond the external and into preexisting love that binds universes.

Cellular Theta Breathing, a meditation technique that promotes expanded states of consciousness will be the topic of

Chapter Seven. This breathing technique will accompany the participants of the retreat, facilitating the expansion of their consciousness throughout their adventure into themselves. An explanation is given and another meditation similar to *Remember Love* will follow.

In Chapter Eight, your vision expands again with the inclusion of the energy of the entire planet, and you awaken to your connection to the collective consciousness or the whole of creation. Expand your consciousness beyond the small self, and into a universal frame of reference known as the Soul, the Higher Self, or the Spirit, taking with you your connection to the people around you as well.

Right after you expand your consciousness beyond anything that you ever thought possible, Chapter Nine explores the crash that you take when your mind reacts to others, making up a fantasy reality. As soon as you obtain an expanded peaceful focus, you are almost immediately tempted to backslide. This process is a normal human tendency, which is the crux of the battle between negative and positive polarities of thought. We take you through this backslide, and back to the connection again.

In Chapter Ten, your view is widened to encompass the duality of reality found in love and fear. Every event is categorized into these two emotions. Your ability to choose and alter the category of the mind is often overlooked. Once you are aware and observing your favorite defenses, as well as touching upon your connection to a greater reality, you are ready to become one with the various parts of yourself. Then you speak. What will you say?

Chapter Eleven is about finding God in the oneness. God would be your God or your Higher Power, because we are not defining your God for you here. We are not promoting a religion, but we are suggesting that God exists and that you can find God everywhere you look, including inside yourself. You will be meeting luminous beings living in the Stars, and as close as your next breath. Who are these angels and what is their mission with you? We will look into the fire and see if you can hear what is being said.

Chapter Twelve is about receiving love. Now we have remembered love, observed love, observed ourselves blocking love and backsliding, integrated love with fear, and it is time to give and receive love. Now that you are inside your heart for this brief time, this is a time of celebration. Receiving the goodness of life is not an automatic process. The willingness to receive peace, love, and compassion involves continued practice in a world of illusions. Giving and receiving are the same, and at this point you experience that truth.

Chapter Thirteen, Beyond Destiny is about Being Peace, the next step upon the path of life. Being Peace is the name of one of the advanced retreats held by Destiny Retreats. It is also the title of yet another book! Remaining in peace is sometimes a minute-by-minute process! This chapter offers suggestions for staying true to your intentions, and moving to a state of abiding peace over and over again.

All along the way, journal questions will follow each chapter so that you may write about your experiences. I encourage you to buy a journal and write your thoughts, emotions, and feelings, right from the very beginning. At the end of the chapters, answer the questions that are provided for additional insight. Later, reread what you have written. You may find many profound answers within your own words that can be found within anyone's book. I hope that the words written here inspire you to find your own wisdom.

Each of these chapters and journal questions builds upon another. They are designed to be a map through the forgetfulness of your adrenaline-based human survival defenses into the peace in the heart. Destiny is an adventure into the remembrance of the safety of your eternal compassionate spirit.

The goal of Destiny is to teach peace through love and compassion. A one-pointed focus on peace, love, and compassion is the most glorious journey you can take. I personally invite you to attend a Destiny Retreat with us. Look for our schedule at www.destinyretreats.com

We are all on the same ship. We are the ship. Welcome Aboard!

Chapter 1 Finding Your Way Home

"Please celebrate me home."
–Celebrate Me Home (James & Loggins, 1977)

"It is no use talking about the 'kingdom of heaven within, if our home is a nest of jarring or thoughtless elements, every member trying to do as he or she likes...to get all they can of pleasure or amusement out of this poor earth, giving nothing back.

"What 1999 will be, whether all these things are the same then as now or worse, or better, depends, of course...upon what we are doing now, or upon what we are not *doing now."*

–Florence Nightingale

(Written after a total solar eclipse of 1873, commenting on the world, as it would be on the August 11, 1999 solar eclipse)

"Say not, 'I have found the truth,' but rather, 'I have found a truth."

–Kahlil Gibran (1883-1931)

"The real power behind whatever success I have now was something I found within myself - something that's in all of us, I think, a little piece of God just waiting to be discovered."

–Tina Turner (1938-)

Wednesday Night

'I feel so alone in this world, distant from all others. There really must be more to life than this, and what about all the suffering in the world? I just don't get it. Surely, there must be more. I guess that is why Janna asked me to go to this retreat with her. She seems so indefinably happier since she went. I wonder if there really is some way to find meaning, and if she has somehow found it, whatever 'it' is, at this Destiny Retreat she went to. Well, I suppose I am going to find out. I feel so uncomfortable about going. If this retreat is supposed to be the place to find inner peace, shouldn't I be feeling peaceful about going?

'It is time for a change in my life. Meditation always sounds like such a good idea. God knows, I need to learn to relax, but going away on a retreat to practice that stuff costs too much money, and takes too much time. How can I justify using my vacation time and money to do this? But I am in a bad mood, depressed, and I just can't put my finger on the problem really. It is like I am empty inside. I just cannot seem to shake this mood, and my best friend is going to this retreat for a second time. She has changed for the better, but I miss, well what do I miss? I guess I miss her feeling like I feel? That is sick, Mel. Oh well, I will just have to make it work. Besides, Janna looks so great after doing this stuff. How hard could it be if she is going back a second time? Why am I always letting her talk me into something? Those retreat people are probably just after your money, and maybe they program you into joining their cult!'

Melanie is a thirty-two year old woman. She keeps saying that she wants to find something more in life, a direction, some meaning, and to learn how to relax. She is uptight, always needing to get everything done just right, but lately she has been really depressed about her life, feeling like she is missing out on something. Now as she packs to leave, her husband Jack is sitting on the corner of their bed, moping around as if he cannot survive four days without her.

Jack is thinking that he doesn't know what to do about her discontent, and feels vaguely responsible. At first, he was reluctant about them spending the money for her to go away without him, but then she seems to need time off, and he would never want to go to one of those kinds of new age mumbo jumbo events. His mind is busy justifying his wife's absence, 'At least her friend Janna has been already, and she looks happier! Anyway, maybe this weekend will help Mel get back to her old self, the one I married. Still, I feel sort of creepy about this whole thing.'

As he watches her agonizing as usual over her perfectionist packing, he asks, "Are you sure you want to go?"

Before she answers, he already knows he should have kept that comment to himself.

Rising up to her defense, she practically yells, "Come on, Jack. We have been through all this. Can't you see that I am trying to pack? If you can't be helpful, then please find something else to do." He leaves the room before she even finishes. She feels justified in her snappy response but worries about him being home alone while she goes off on this crazy adventure with Janna. As her head is still wobbling side to side in a justified little dance, she thinks, 'Sure, Janna doesn't have a husband! She can just trot off anytime she wants to since she has no one that it affects! But enough of this, I need to pack.'

'How much stuff do I need to take on this trip? What if it gets too cold? I'm always cold. Better take a few sweaters. Where will I sleep? Why do I need a sleeping bag? I have to have my own room because I will not be comfortable with people that I don't know. Thank God I'm riding with someone I know! I will room with her. What will they have to eat and drink?' Her mind anxiously agonizes over every detail so much so that she doesn't even notice that her body is as tight as a drum.

'Wait a minute. Where is that packing list? Here it is, and what? No caffeine when I want it? What will I ever do without diet soda to drink? I need it to function. No chocolate! I better just sneak a few snacks into my bag. No smoking, that's a laugh!

'No way! I do not need a bathing suit. No way will I be wearing a bathing suit. I am way too fat and too self-conscious to wear a bathing suit around all those perfect strangers. I will just forget that item and then I won't be able to use it, even if I am asked to wear it. Ha!

'OK, all packed. I better try to sleep because six o'clock in the morning comes early. Why do we need a pad and a sleeping bag? Oh well, I wish I had packed yesterday, but it's too late now.' She runs to the kitchen for some contraband and grabs a bigger bag from the garage, big enough to store a twelve-pack of diet, caffeine-laden soda, cigarettes, chocolate, and a few other snacks just in case the food is appalling.

Returning to the bedroom, where Jack is now crawling into bed, she meticulously moves the stuff from the original bag into the new one. She carefully places all her clothing on top of her stash at the bottom of her suitcase, closes it, and dresses for bed. Painstakingly, she picks out her clothes for the morning as her mind continues to run amok. Finally, she sets her alarm clock for six o'clock in the morning. Melanie's poor tired body is ready to retire for the night, but her mind has other plans.

Thursday Morning

'Four o'clock and I have been tossing and turning all night. I thought I would feel peaceful about going to a peaceful retreat.

Why am I so nervous about going on a little retreat in a beautiful place? Calm down and rest! Oh, forget it! I might as well get up and recheck my stuff. Why do we leave so early when the thing does not start until late afternoon? How can a six-hour trip take eight hours or more? I just do not get it?'

Jack tosses and moans as if her anxiety is also disturbing his sleep. 'Poor guy, he needs his sleep for work today. Go to sleep.' But she doesn't sleep. She is thinking and thinking.

Melanie's body gets no rest because of a mind that is anxiously going over every detail of her upcoming adventure into relaxation! It hardly seems fair. And time goes on with her thinking and thinking, and double checking her last minute worries about leaving her house for a couple of days.

'Seven o'clock and my ride is still not here. Good grief, this is nerve-racking! I wonder if I am the only one this nervous. Oh, there she is!'

Now that she hears a car, her worrying does not cease. Melanie really does not notice that her physical body is seriously suffering from stress, because she usually feels quite tense. Tension has become her natural state of being. Her shoulders are tight and her stomach is queasy. Eating was out of the question but coffee, her usual fuel, is making her too nauseous to stomach for once. 'Tension and lack of sleep make me feel like throwing up. Oh great, that feeling on top of a long ride!'

"Hi, Janna," Melanie says, looking and sounding positively cheerful, a well-used façade.

Janna is not fooled by Melanie's happy face, since her shoulders are so tense they look like earmuffs instead of shoulders; and is that a green tinge to her skin?

"Hi, Mel!"

Melanie is Janna's best friend in this world. She is one of those people who will always come through for you when you really need a friend. She is totally dependable. Today, she is relieved to have her best friend coming along to the retreat, sharing one of the best experiences she has ever had. 'The one thing that I have worried about when I have been personally transforming myself is that my friends will be left behind.'

No sooner does the thought escape her mind before she realizes that Melanie is just saying goodbye to her husband. 'Oh, she probably feels that way about her husband! Worrying about your husband not understanding this type of meaning and experience is even scarier than what I have been worried about. Wow! I was so busy selfishly wanting her to join me that I forgot how it might affect her relationship with Jack. I wish I had worked on getting him to come with us. Darn it! Well, I will help her get him to come next time if she likes it as much as I did. I know she is going to love it. She hasn't been very happy lately, and it's like she's in a big rut. I mean, well, why haven't they had a baby yet? It's been long enough. What is she afraid of?

'If only she really just participates to the fullest, I know she will get through whatever sadness she has and get on with her life. What if she doesn't like it? What if... I have got to quit doing the retreat for her! What's wrong with me? I am happy to have my best friend share this unbelievable experience with me, and now I am worried? Let it go, Janna. Just talk about iced tea and the weather, all the fair weather topics on the way to the retreat. Stay off anything too serious.'

"Hey Mel, let's get something to eat on the way out of town. You look hungry."

The car ride is spent chatting about work and other activities that occupy their way too busy lives. Occasionally, Melanie asks Janna about the retreat, the food, the rooms, and other details, and Janna being a very good former participant, gives vague but what she thinks reassuring answers. The answers to the questions are not all that reassuring to Melanie, primarily because of the vagueness. She is left feeling moderately anxious, as if Janna is hiding something from her. In reality, Janna is just trying to ensure that her best friend gets to have the full experience and not ruin the surprises for her. But Janna feels tired from this ongoing withholding, questioning game. She didn't realize that it would be so hard to drive Mel to this event.

The supposedly short road trip becomes one long trip of many stops for food, the bathroom, to shop, and to take a picture of the breathtaking scenery. Finally, they stop for the fifth time. This time, they have a sandwich before finishing the ride to the retreat site. Melanie's mind continues to wander throughout the ride.

'This car trip hasn't been so bad and we did have a little time to shop along the way. And oh my gosh, what a beautiful place! I already feel more peaceful, but what is going to happen when we get there? You know, maybe I will really try to follow the rules about use of excessive caffeine and smoking. Cigarettes and caffeine leave a bad taste in my mouth anyway. Maybe I could use this time to quit!' A long sigh falls from her mouth and she admits to herself, 'I really want to feel different, to feel like I have a direction and not waste the money I am spending, not to mention the time I am spending away from Jack. Just relax. How bad can it be?'

Later that day, they finally arrive at the site after a jerky ride down a dusty unpaved road. As they enter the building, the stress of the ride and the anxiety of facing the unknown are almost unbearable for Melanie. Janna, on the other hand, looks consumed with bliss and relief to be here.

In front of the meeting room, a couple of women converse with a man sitting at a table full of electronic equipment. Another woman is walking toward them, inviting them to make themselves comfortable. The participants are invited to take a seat in a circle and relax. She offers them a drink of water and a nametag. A familiar and relaxing song begins to play.

When the song ends, one of the women in front of the room says, "Close your eyes. Take a deep relaxing breath. We are going to begin with a guided meditation." Heavenly music softly begins to play, and a woman's soft comforting voice begins with the first guided meditation of the retreat.

Finding Your Way Home
(© Cornelius & Donovan-Vaughn, 1996)

"Take several deep breaths and clear your thoughts. Imagine that it is a beautiful spring day. The golden white sunlight embraces you. You are walking next to a small stream that winds its way across a beautiful green valley. Hear the water as it soothingly bubbles across small stones. The water is clear and you see tiny fish darting about. Smell the fragrance of wild flowers, and the rich musty scent of the warm earth. A soothing cool breeze caresses your skin while the sunlight warms you, creating the perfect balance. As you breathe in, the air feels cool. As you breathe out, the air warms. Up ahead, you see a powerful mountain arising out of the valley floor. This beautiful mountain magically beckons to you in some unexplainable way from deep within. Your heartbeat quickens with excitement as you walk toward the base of the mountain. Breathe naturally. Feel the cooling and warming of your rhythmic breathing. Breathe into the center of your being and relax. You feel good here. You sense this is a place of power. As you reach the base of the mountain, see how it towers above you. Feel and sense the mountain's energy. Create your perfect mountain. You know you will be climbing soon, and anticipation surges through you. Continue to let your breath be in the center of your being. Breath is light. It is the source of energy. Look at the mountain again. This mountain is the mountain of your life.

It symbolizes your journey of enlightenment. It symbolizes your mission in life. Take a moment in silence and give thanks for your life and your mission.

"Now you are ready to begin your journey. First, you must prepare for the long climb by lightening your load. Sit down in the grass under a tree and ask yourself, "What do I need to leave behind of my physical self, my physical nature, or my physical attachments in order to undertake the journey up the mystical mountain?" Take a moment in silence and perform a sacred ceremony saying to yourself, "I now leave this excess weight behind in order to continue my journey into my true nature and be enlightened." See yourself releasing these physical limitations and allowing them to flow into the ground and disappear. Breathe deeply.

"Now, continue walking along the winding trail. Look up at the clouds drifting across the azure sky. As you walk, you feel the dirt under your feet, and the path becomes steeper. You are walking on a spiraling trail that winds around the mountain all the way to the summit. You come to a place a quarter of the way to the top. You see a plateau where you can sit. Draw a circle in the dirt with your hand and sit within the sacred wheel. Feel at one with the earth inside this circle. Ask yourself, "What do I need to leave behind of my emotional self in order to continue my journey into my true nature and be enlightened?" Trust your intuitive voice to help you and listen to the answers. Perform a scared ceremony of letting go, saying to yourself, "I now leave these emotions behind and I will remember what I have left here." Take a moment in silence to release these emotions. Allow them to flow into the earth and disappear. Breathe deeply.

"Now, continue walking. As you climb higher, the air becomes thinner. Breathe deeply the cool crisp air and feel the energy flowing in. You are beginning to feel clearer inside yourself. You keep walking, though it is difficult until you get

halfway up the trail. You come to a place where there is a large cool boulder. This place feels like a good place to rest. You sit down with your back against this boulder, feeling the coolness of the stone. The power of this rock permeates your body and you feel one with the solidity of this stone. Gaze out at the horizon and see the lush green valley below. The tiny stream looks like a sliver ribbon. Ask yourself, "What thoughts are blocking me? What mental walls do I have? What do I need to release to continue my journey into my true nature and be enlightened?" Let your heart be your guide on the path of releasing old fears, worries, resentments, or any other thoughts you no longer need. Perform a sacred ceremony of letting go, saying to yourself, "I now leave these thoughts and I will remember what I have left here." See yourself releasing all blocks occurring on an intellectual level that keep you from being enlightened. Allow them to flow into the ground and disappear. Breathe deeply.

"Now, continue walking, feeling rested, and focusing on every step because the trail is narrow and very steep. You now have greater and greater confidence and joy as you reach a place just below the peak of the mountain. There is a rock ledge where you can rest and dangle your feet over the valley far below. Sit on this ledge and feel the power of this place. Feel yourself as that power. Listening to you own inner wisdom, ask yourself, "What old beliefs do I need to let go of to fully experience my true spiritual self and be enlightened?" Listen to the answer and perform the sacred ceremony of letting go again. Allow these old limiting beliefs to flow into the ground and disappear. Finally, you feel a sense of joy and release. You stand up, back away from the ledge and notice that your head is so high that it is almost in the clouds that surround the top of your mountain. Take a moment in silence to feel this new sense of inner peace. Breathe deeply.

"With eager anticipation, you finish climbing the trail. You

are now standing on the top of your mountain. Look around in all directions. The air is colder up here. An eagle flies close by. Smile as you feel one with the eagle, and as you see farther than you have ever seen before. This mountain is the mountain of every day. You climb your mountain every day. You are on this path, this journey of the mystical mountain. Look around. The ground sparkles with pieces of mica. Smell the fragrance of the flowers as you lean over and touch the petals. Be one with everything in your sight, the clean air, and the evergreen trees around you, the animals and the mountain. See the ground as a very special vision of light and of beauty unlike anything you have ever seen before. Keep this vision and hold it in your heart. See rainbow colors everywhere. Let the rays of the sun enter your heart. As you hold the vision, I want you to hear a prayer forming in your heart. "This is a prayer for harmony, peace, and love." Trust your inner guidance. Trust harmony, balance. Trust that you will remember what is necessary to let go of. Trust love.

"Slowly, begin your walk down the mountain, repeating your prayer in the silence of your heart. Walking down the spiraling trail is much easier. You hold your beautiful vision of joy, knowing that this joy is always available, and that you are one with the universe. As you pass each area where you rested and released, you touch the vision to your heart and give thanks. As you reach the lower part of the mountain, you look out over the lengthening shadows that lace the floor of the valley. You watch the sun steadily lowering behind the horizon. Now you are enthusiastic to get home before dark. When you have reached level ground, let your focus be on your body. Take several deep, cleansing breaths. Feel the love and joy in your heart and at your own pace, slowly open your eyes."

So we begin the journey of finding your way home, to acknowledge your purpose in life, to expand your consciousness, to guide your life down the path that fills you with meaning, and to experience states of bliss and finally enlightenment. This journey will take you from the anxious and lost feeling of Melanie, and hopefully to the just awakened state of Janna, and beyond and beyond. Since the journey never ends, it matters not where you are on the path. Asleep, barely awake, or fully awake, this journey is an infinite journey. All paths lead home, some quicker, some more blissfully than others.

What is the difference between Janna and Melanie? One is still sleeping and the other is awakening to an unlimited world of creation. We will follow these two women along the path toward their inner home, the path of aligning with, and creating their destiny. As you follow this path, you will be finding parts of yourself that you have lost, as well as finding excess garbage that weighs you down on your daily journey. You can begin realigning yourself with your higher purpose as you adjust your thoughts, emotions, feelings, and actions to create your destiny. So no matter where you are, this journey is heading your way.

Let's start at the beginning. Your current life is a journey that you are taking every day, every second. Even before you climb out of bed, you are creating your life. Let's imagine that when you awaken this morning, you remember a dream. The dream could be that you are late for a test in a crucial class, but you have forgotten where the class is located. You are naked and when you finally find the class, the test is over. An annoying bell is ringing, which signals to students that the class is finished. You failed the class because you missed the test. Then you wake up to the sound of the alarm blaring in your head, maybe even cursing it when you punch down the snooze alarm. As you lie there half asleep and half awake; that dreamy delicious brainwave state in which your senses delight in the restful comfort of your bed, you shake free of the anxiety that created your failure, laugh a little about the alarm being incorporated into your dream, and tell yourself that it is time to get up any second. The thought of getting up and going to work does not appeal to you very much today, and maybe it is like that much of the time. The alarm sounds again and up you go. You think that you are awake, but maybe you are still sleepwalking, like one of many in our world today. Twice you were awakened by the alarm and you may still be sleeping! Right now, the alarm is going off. You are on a journey to find your way home.

If you are lucky, during moments of clarity, you may notice that you are creating your life as you momentarily wake up and look around. But who in this busy world has much time even for a moment to observe their life. It is easier to follow the road that is of least resistance, and fall back into sleepwalking, and yet this easy road often feels quite meaningless, leading you in circles with rare movements forward. When you are awake, you will see that you are heading down a path. All paths lead you home. You have a choice to wake up and chart your course, to notice your direction, to be awake on your journey.

Everyone has a destiny. You are creating it every minute. Destiny is the future that is just outside of your awareness. Your destiny is being created right now as you read. This book is becoming part of your destiny! Every thought that you have every second is creating your future. When you decide to focus your energy, thoughts, and feelings on your goals, you become the captain of your ship. Focus your energy and your life will magically transform. But even before you can focus, you have to notice what you are doing right now. Then, you have to notice that you don't really know what goal will actually make you happy. You may think that some obsession outside of you will make you happy, but will it really work? Or will you be endlessly pursuing more and more items? Seeking possessions or experiences is a path, and every path will lead you home. Eventually, when you reach a saturation point, you will figure it out. Home is inside. Looking outside to find your home can feel empty and meaningless.

Celebrate Me Home (James & Loggins, 1977)

Melanie is already beginning to notice the music at the retreat. The music is chosen very carefully to promote the journey she is taking. As you read along, you will benefit from listening to inspiring sounds. Music is a gift that will be with our participants all along the way on their journey. What Melanie doesn't know yet is that she is going to be emotionally moved over and over by a musical score provided by the staff of the retreat. Since you are reading and don't have our soundtrack, you will be providing the music for your life. To begin the conscious creation of your reality, finding your way home, you can begin by consciously creating a musical score to accompany your life.

What songs would be the perfect ones to represent your life up to this point? Like many people, you probably have more than one song for more than one time and event, and the list grows as you age. Wait a minute! If your music is all very negative and depressing, then your music is reflecting how you think, and reflecting how you create reality. Just like in the movies, you decide to consciously set your life's adventures to music and to every other choice you are making every day. Music profoundly affects your mood, health (Emoto, 2006), and your motivation. Imagine right now how you would feel if inspiring, energizing songs were always playing in the background as if you are the star in a movie. If your life were perfect right now, what song would be playing? As you continue with your reading, allow some music to play in the background too. The music will encourage you in creating your destiny. What song would be playing right now? Who is in charge of your music? Take charge now!

What song is playing now? What purpose will music serve for you? Music connects your brain to your heart. Pick some music that you would use to inspire the world to choose love, peace, and compassion. Music mirrors your mood and follows you through life, no matter what your life may be. In the beginning of your life, you hear a lullaby and riddles. Lullabies echo a time long gone and follow you into the future. The words no longer make any sense, but they continue to inspire love and the peaceful sleep of the small child.

The nursery rhymes you sing to your children contain mythical, ancient wisdom, and sometimes the lyrics can teach which direction to take if you listen.

"Mary had a little lamb. Its fleece was white as snow. Everywhere that Mary went, the lamb was sure to go." (Thomas Edison 1837-1941)

"Row, row, row your boat gently down the stream. Merrily, merrily, merrily, life is but a dream." (English Nursery Rhyme) Listen to the meaning.

Later, your songs are songs of holidays and celebrations. You pick special songs for people you love. You repeat the words of your favorite songs over and over and over as a teenager until your parents would love to buy earplugs. Music echoes the intensity of your emotions at turbulent times in your life. You marry with a special song. What has happened to your music along the way? Through music, you may still remember your home inside. Music is one way you still remember the compassion that dwells in your heart. Choose the music to bring you to the remembrance of this indwelling compassion.

In fall one year, I attended a wedding in an ancient chapel. Tall, stained-glass windows allowed shafts of light to shimmer into the congregation. Seated at the front of the podium on a tall wooden stool, a beautiful Irish woman softly strummed her guitar. Her flaming red hair draped alongside the guitar and her emerald dress flowed to the ground as if an extension of the light striking her from above. Just as the mother of the bride began her ascent down the aisle, the words of the song begin, "You are the wind beneath my wings" (Henley & Silbar, 1983). A bride's tribute to her mother became the tears of that setting in that momentary space of time.

Songs are at church and on the street. They are everywhere, and accompany your memories and beliefs. They are at the play in kindergarten when your child, the star, sings on top of the Christmas tree. They are at your death and your birth. When you hear a sentimental song, the person with whom you were with when you first heard that melody floods into your heart, and time stands still.

Music opens the heart. The songs are songs of compassion, and there are so many songs that you could feel that your heart will expand beyond its capacity, but fortunately, there is no such thing.

It can frighten you to open your heart. Why? Forget about asking why questions, and ask how to stop the fear. We will traverse the path through fear later on in the book. For now, look back in time to find an answer. The fear to be within the heart can only be present because you learned to be afraid at a very young age, and you learned to close the heart to protect it. Music reminds you to open your heart once more and find the goodness that exists beneath ordinary reality.

Angels sing to you. Turn on the radio. Play a CD. Load up your MP3 player. Find the music of the heart so that your heart can remain open enough to glimpse peace. Let the music take you home to the love inside your heart. Music can heal your soul and lead you to companionship with others. Without thought, music can inspire you to be close to others. Music inspires depression and anger, but it can also inspire you to forget the thoughts of negativity and fill you with hope. It is your choice to allow music to lift your life.

If you focus on a beautiful song instead of the negative programs, stories of chaos and other sensational news that so readily fills our ears, then you will find your way home. Remember that the news is filled with stories of the unusual, and does not in any way reflect what is actually happening all around you. If you are looking for a quick fix to your life, tune out the negative news, and tune into all of the angels singing. Shift your view. Shift your sound. Listen and you will hear the voice of love all around you.

What if all you heard was love?

JOURNAL ACTIVITY – *Journal Instructions*:

As you read the pages of the book, I suggest that you keep a journal. The thoughts of the mind are very quick. If you continue reading when you have a thought, emotion, or feeling on a subject, you may forget to notice what is happening for you. Your reaction to emotional information can be to distract! Write about any strong reactions, especially negative thoughts and intense emotions that you have. While you are at it, notice how your body feels when you are thinking negative, and what emotions are occurring as well.

Using a journal will help you to stay focused on what is occurring internally, while you investigate how you create your life. Write about your mind talk. Notice the topics of obsessions of your mind. When you record the thoughts of your mind, start to notice the theme of your mind's preoccupation. Does your mind think happy thoughts? Does your mind think thoughts that depress you or make you anxious? Is your mind constantly trying to analyze others, or maybe it is constantly judging others? Notice time in your thoughts. Are you in the past, present, or future? Keeping the mind in the present drastically improves your life immediately.

Is your mind judging you, and are you in turn judging your mind talk? If you are judging your mind, then record those judgments. Observe what your mind is doing and record some of the thoughts that affect you the most. Especially record desires that you may have that distract you from noticing what you are thinking and feeling. For example, you are reading a passage in the book or reading a journal question and suddenly, you decide to have a snack, smoke a cigarette, etc. Later, you notice that you stopped reading or writing at a certain point. That point is a topic on which to journal.

You might benefit now by reading chapter one again, and stopping to record significant thoughts that you had while reading. Be sure to record negative reactions. These negative reactions are your records of fear.

The journal is for you to slow down the reactions that you have so that you can identify your underlying beliefs. The journal is an aid in your meditation; an observation of your life. It is a place to record your intentions, and to help you understand how you are creating your destiny!

OK, let's look at a journal exercise for you. Journals will be discussed in a little more detail later, but for now, find a journal and start answering these questions.

Chapter One Journal Questions

1. What kind of future do you want to create?
2. What thoughts, emotions, and feelings do you have about the prospect of your future, and how do you feel about dwelling on the future rather than the present?
3. If your music, activities, thoughts, emotions, and feelings seem to contradict the future that you envision, then how will

you alter them? (Hint: positively correct any statements right now.)
4. What music is playing in your life? How will you change the music?
5. What music would be playing if your destiny were one of peace, love, and compassion?
6. Record your mind talk as often as possible! Observation is the first step in finding your way home.

Chapter 2 Who Are You?

"I am prepared to meet anyone, but whether anyone is prepared for the great ordeal of meeting me is another matter."
–Mark Twain (1835-1910)

"This is our purpose: to make as meaningful as possible this life that has been bestowed upon us; to live in such a way that we may be proud of ourselves; to act in such a way that some part of us lives on."
–Oswald Spengler (1880-1936)

'Well, here we are! The first meditation was OK, I guess, since I slept through half of it. I wonder if other people fall asleep during the meditations. Am I the only one?' Melanie is agonizing again. 'I hope I didn't snore or do anything stupid like drool.'

Just then, the facilitator begins to tell the group that they are about to go around the room and introduce themselves. They are seated in a circular arrangement.

"Tell the group anything you would like about yourself that you feel is relevant, and what you would like to accomplish while you are here," she states serenely, like it would be the simplest of tasks for anyone to do.

'Oh no, we are going to have to talk in front of all these people and tell them why we are here. Let's see, why am I here anyway? I was pressured by my friend, Janna? Ha! I better come up with something serious or I might look stupid. I am sure everyone else is here to become a better person, or already knows all about this meditation, breathing stuff. Oh yeah, that's why I wanted to come too. I want to find more meaning in my life. That sounds good enough, but what can I say about myself? I am thirty-three years old and still haven't had a baby, don't like my job, and sometimes wonder if my marriage is going to last. I can't say that stuff. It's too personal. I will just say that sometimes I wonder what I am doing with my life. That's safe.'

Melanie had a moment of rest during the meditation but has immediately been overtaken by anxiety afterwards. She doesn't even notice how strange it really is to fall asleep in a room full of strangers, when quite often, she cannot sleep in the comfort of her own bed. In fact, she never even takes naps. Oh yes, she has also missed most of what everyone else is saying because she is too busy obsessing about her own upcoming performance.

Janna, on the other hand, is still looking relaxed, and even happy. But she is a little nervous about Mel's experience and her inner dialogue is also making her a little tense. 'What if she hates it? What if she has a bad time, and worse what if she just doesn't get it? Poor Mel. I know she wants a baby but what's holding her back? She seems to be happily married but they don't really do anything different, day-in-day-out. It's like they are in some kind of rut for crying out loud. They are so young to be so set in their ways. Most people have children when they are happily married for as long as they have been. She is always saying how much she wants children. Something is always holding her back. Who am I to talk? I'm worse than her, not married and... wait a minute. I was peaceful one minute ago, and now I am beating myself up and worrying about someone else. I better journal this mind talk as soon as I get a chance. Breathe and relax, Janna. Get in the present.'

Melanie has no way to stop her mind and it rants on and on, stopping only to share her somewhat superficial reason for coming, to find more meaning in life. 'That sharing activity wasn't so bad. Some of those other people actually look more nervous than me. And that woman, Deanna, she has some nerve telling the whole group she is an addict. Whoa, I would be mortified to tell all these strangers that I was that out of control. How can she be so. . . well, I don't like her. She bugs me really. At least I don't have to spend much time around her. Thankfully, I am not the only one that is a little insecure about being here. But good grief, at least I am not working on addiction problems. I don't have anything that bad to work on here like Deanna. If you have to be that screwed up to be here, I wonder why Janna thinks we need to be here. But then, the lady brought her daughter and that married couple that came together, I don't think that Jack would ever think about. . .'

That couple Melanie is talking about are Susan and Darryl, who are actually attending this retreat to improve their marriage. They were told by another friend of theirs that Destiny is great for couples, increases intimacy, helps couples set mutual goals, and to get on the same track. They already have a great marriage, but are the kind of people that want to keep it that way, and know that a good marriage - like anything in life - takes time and energy to maintain.

"I put my energy into what I love," said Darryl when he shared, and several of the women in the room sighed. If it was a script meant to impress the crowd, it was a good one. The couple sit cozily snuggled next to each other as if they really are very comfortably in love with each other after fifteen years of marriage. Susan says that getting away from the kids with her husband for a retreat like this is a way to keep their marriage a number one priority in her life, because otherwise they could let their kids, jobs, and multiple activities overshadow any relationship they ever had as a couple. They also commented that they would love to bring their teenagers next time, after realizing that teens attend with their parents as well. But this time was just for the two of them, Susan and Darryl both agree.

The parent they have noticed is Sophia, who brought her sixteen-year-old daughter, Madison. They are attending because Sophia wanted to bring her daughter back after she came to the retreat once before. She would like her daughter to have this experience early in life, long before she makes her important life choices. Madison shyly states that she is here because her mother dragged her to the retreat. Everyone laughs because she is smiling when she makes the comment.

"No, really I wanted to see what my mom was talking about when she came home. She looked like she had joined a new church; she was so happy and different for a while. Then, she had some trouble. Well, I wanted to see her that happy again and I thought maybe I would like to see what happened here too. But she did sort of drag me when I told her I wanted to know why she changed, and when I told her she wasn't as happy as when she first came back. So here I am."

Deanna, as Melanie noticed, said that she is here to continue working on recovery. She told the group that she is in a twelve-step program and her recovery is the most important part of her life. She is here to work on herself.

"I have been in recovery for ten years and feel that it is important to learn as many coping skills as I can find to help me with my program." Deanna is very comfortable sharing because she has regularly been attending Alcoholic Anonymous meetings for many years. However, she is a bit unsettled by some negative energy she feels from Melanie. She thinks that Melanie is immensely stuck up and someone to avoid.

As the participants go around the room, they are obviously put on the spot and some are nervous about speaking. This is their second chance to express why they came to the retreat. The first chance was when they filled out their enrollment form on which they were asked what they would like to accomplish at the retreat. The objective of this line of questioning is to get the person to a point where they can eventually state an intention, some goal they desire to create, which will be happening soon. Every time they are asked the intention question, their mind is forced to decide what they want in life. At this point, some are still vague like Madison, while others are very pointed like Susan. But over time, many of the intentions will transform.

The participants and facilitators have also gone over some ground rules for the retreat at this point. These rules are designed to help the participants have a safe and productive experience. As with any rules, however, the mind may have thoughts about whether or not it will be constrained by the rules set forth. Rules can create both inner and outer conflict, demonstrating how one deals with authority. With these conflicts in mind, the participants have already been given a journal with journal questions; the first is regarding these rules as well as their reaction to the first meditation.

Melanie, our nervous participant with premeditated plans to break the guidelines in the packing list, balks right away about the new agreements that she finds in her journal after they were stated by the facilitator. 'Stay conscious the whole time? Does that mean when I fell asleep, I broke a rule? Stay silent? Why? Be on time? Rules and more rules! I should be late just to... Well, anyway, if I get a headache, I am drinking my diet soda! And I AM EATING MY CHOCOLATE!'

Madison thinks the time rule is funny, because she cannot figure out how her mother did the seminar before when her mother has never been on time in her life. 'Well, she will be on time with me here because I am NOT walking in late because of her!'

Deanna did not hear the rules because she was busy reading forward in the journal while the rules were being read.

All the others have their various reactions from none to complete disregard to missing the whole activity because their mind was elsewhere. The entire activity, after all, only lasted a couple of minutes and that is no time at all for a mind to wander away and miss what was said.

Chapter Two Journal Questions

1. How did you get this book and start reading it, what purpose did you have in mind? What would you like to accomplish by reading this information?
2. When put on the spot to tell others about yourself and your goals, what happens to you?
3. How do you react when someone gives you a set of rules to follow such as being on time?
4. If you have a problem with rules, what are you feeling about them in your body, in your emotions, and what thoughts do you have concerning them?
5. If you do not have a problem with rules, how do you feel, think, and what emotions do you have about rules or about people who break them?

Chapter 3 Silent Consciousness

"In the attitude of silence the soul finds the path in a clearer light, and what is elusive and deceptive resolves itself into crystal clearness. Our life is a long and arduous quest after Truth."

–Mahatma Gandhi (1869 - 1948)

"Happiness is that state of consciousness which proceeds from the achievement of one's values."

–Ayn Rand (1905 - 1982)

"Silence promotes the presence of God, prevents many harsh and proud words, and suppresses many dangers in the way of ridiculing or harshly judging our neighbors...If you are faithful in keeping silence when it is not necessary to speak, God will preserve you from evil when it is right for you to talk."

–Francois Fenelon (1651-1715)

Staying Conscious

Finally, one of the facilitators begins the goal of presenting an explanation, after the beginning introductions and housekeeping chores have been completed.

"Welcome to Destiny. By simply showing up here, you have taken your first step on a new path. We call this journey finding your way home. The home is the place you have never left, but one you may have forgotten. Home is you. Home is me. Home is all of us. Prepare yourself to awaken. It is your choice, of course, but hopefully, you will choose to never fall so fast asleep again as you may have been up to now. Of course, you cannot change a lifetime of habits with one long weekend retreat, but you can fine-tune which direction you will be heading in your life. Then, all you have to do is to keep remembering your intention, your focus.

"It may appear in the beginning of this experience called Destiny that we will be structuring much of your time during this journey. However, the experience you have at this retreat will be of your own creation. We are here as way-showers or guides through your journey of self-discovery. Destiny is a creation. It is your creation. This experience will be one of many calls you have had and will have to remember to wake up. You would not be here if you were not ready.

"It is our belief that we are all in search of ecstasy in this life, ecstasy in one form or another. And another word for this common search for ecstasy could be called dysfunction. Dysfunction is the search for ecstasy. It is what people think they are doing in their search for happiness. If your true home is inside, then you are misguided looking for ecstasy in the world. You are looking in the all the wrong places, and maybe you are lost, sleepwalking through life.

"Think about the ways in which you search for happiness. These stimulations might be called work, sex, drugs, alcohol, food, gambling, money, shopping, or other people in the form of relationships. When these activities are used as a search for happiness, they all have a very common result: they do not work! Oh yes, they may feel good for a minute or an hour. They may take the place of a real life for a while. But if something really worked, you would only have to do it once and it would last forever.

"Are you achieving happiness by living a distraction life? Are you using substitutions in life as a necessary prerequisite to even participating in life? Are you waiting for something to happen, maybe before you can be happy? We use these outside forces over and over and over again, constantly hoping they will bring us happiness. We hope beyond hope that these external solutions will solve our internal yearning for completion. But in fact, you are keeping yourself occupied and fooled into thinking you are almost happy. You will be as soon as you get one more time, one more bang, one more some satisfaction out there that the world will give you if you get lucky, right?

"No, you are just distracted and forgetting where to find fulfillment. And you are caught up seeking the next fix out there in the world so that you don't even know that you are looking in the wrong direction. You may even have heard that the Bible says, "Happiness is within." But you may not know what that means. You have been on a journey your whole life for ecstasy derived from a source outside of your self. As long as you are looking for external solutions for happiness, you are lost!

"From this point forward on this journey, you will be observing yourself in your search for what you call life, and you will be observing your creations. OBSERVATION OF YOURSELF IS A KEY TO ENLIGHTENMENT. Observe your mind. Observe your actions and your reactions! It is the part of your mind often called the ego that seeks for happiness outside of yourself. It is this part of you; your ego-mind that thinks that controlling your external environment will result in internal happiness. Your ego-mind filters everything you experience, and your ego-mind is a system that is based largely on survival. The brain is very focused on survival! It is not focused on internal happiness, or even really that concerned with things that are outside of its little area of interest! Your ego-mind bases its decisions on cellular memories of this lifetime of experiences;

the ones that have been coming in from your senses. It remembers what it thinks is important and bases its decisions on the past and on survival. The brain wants to keep you safe and alive. It is most likely doing a terrific job. However, the brain's obsessions may be blocking your satisfaction.

"Think about your memory for a moment. Memory is the past. And yet it is the current filter through which all your new thoughts must pass. In this way, your past becomes your present. Everything in your life right this moment was created by what you did in your past. Your present is creating your future. It is in this way that your past creates your future. Your future is your destiny, and it can all be based on your brain's survival instincts if you keep allowing it to stay that way. You are creating your destiny today. Right here, right now, you are constantly in the process of creating your destiny. What are you thinking about right now? What are you doing? Your current thoughts are creating your destiny.

"IT IS POSSIBLE FOR YOU TO BE MORE THAN YOUR MEMORY, MORE THAN JUST SURVIVAL, MORE THAN JUST DISTRACTIONS!

"At the retreat, the tool for understanding how you create your destiny is to stay in the present. Through observation, you can begin to recognize when you are being motivated or being directed by your past or by your survival needs. To help you stay present, you will be implementing the process of BEING SILENT and OBSERVING the present moment. SILENCE IS A KEY TO ENLIGHTENMENT. You are going to minimize your distractions and thus assist in your ability to watch yourself create your destiny. You are going on a journey into silence so that you may minimize your escapes, minimize your distractions, and minimize your survival instincts."

Right now, let's take a break in this facilitator's introduction about staying conscious and silent, and check in with our favorite participant's mind chatter for a minute and see what's going on in their heads after hearing about the idea of silence.

'Now what? Silence... for how long?' Melanie is positively rebellious again. You would never know that she is actually a very organized person, one who likes all her ducks in a row. Her mind talks like a three-year-old who will never be told what to do or when. The problem with Melanie is that she likes control, but does not like others to be in control of her life. Melanie is a control freak because she has so much fear. She doesn't know she is afraid because she is so accustomed to keeping her life in order and to being tense that she hardly ever notices that she cannot stand anything different. Silence just might make Melanie notice how out of control she really is in her life. She cannot have what she wants because she cannot stand any change whatsoever. If she were to observe her body, her emotions, and her thoughts, she would find so much tension, negativity, and fear that she would be shocked into an epiphany of understanding. 'Well, I doubt I will be able to be quiet in a room with my best friend for three days. Why would anyone want to have that much silence anyway?'

As the facilitator explains that for the next day or two, the whole group of participants is to be silent, and gives an explanation about why, part of this explanation is missed when the minds of the participants are reacting to the news. Their unique reactions could actually be used to symbolize their whole way of creating reality. The way the mind reacts is the way the mind has been programmed by its environment, along with its genetic brain chemistry. In other words, reactions develop using your mind in contact with your world throughout a lifetime.

Janna is feeling relief at the moment. 'Now, at least, Mel cannot vent her frustrations at me for the next couple of days. Hopefully, she will be in a much better frame of mind when she can talk again. I hope she is going to say thank you for dragging me here. Surely she will get it. I just hope she doesn't go into that nasty judgmental attitude if someone happens to talk during the silence.' Janna is again invested in her friend's experience, feeling responsible for the outcome. She wants Melanie to be happier, and hopes she has helped her with this goal, in fact she feels that she is risking rejection for trying to be helpful. Janna's mind is also giving her a hard time!

And Now for a Moment or a Few Days of Silence

Why silence? One of the most distracting activities in our life is talking. It is a paradoxical situation that all these casually spouted words are actually helping to create our reality, and consequently our destiny. Words are often used to express our worry, negativity, and lack to others. Listen very carefully to the words you hear every day of your life. Listen to the words you hear coming out of your mouth. Listen to the words you hear in your mind. Many of these words are fear-based, filled with anxiety. They contain worry. Ever since the beginning of the book, we have been eavesdropping on the mental chatter of the participants. Think about the themes of some of these words, and notice how they are weaving realities into being. It is easier to see the way others create reality many times than the way we are creating it. Our mind often deceives us, fogs us over so that we are not noticing what we are doing, where we are going, and how we are making our lives function.

Experiencing silence, even if you can only do it for a few seconds, has many purposes. The very first goal is to stop your conversational distraction. Even if you can't stay quiet and you start talking to someone, you might just wonder why you had to say something when you are attempting to be silent.

Another purpose of silence is to give you a chance to better observe your mind talking and to notice your concerns. If you spent one week writing all of your mind talk, you would probably have a book, but wouldn't it be repetitive? The mind has only a few topics that it drones on and on about, which brings us to a new suggestion. While watching your mind talk, begin compiling a list of the themes it uses. The theme might be worry. The theme might be a substance, like money, food, etc. It might be about doing, doing, doing. It might be about judgment of others. It might be about the future, and it might be about the past. My favorite themes concern money, health, and relationships. By the way, my themes are usually negative and anxious, which means that my brain chemistry is naturally anxiously depressed. This condition is manageable. Try being silent and observing your mind. Watch what happens very carefully. Write about it.

One of the major goals at Destiny is to alter your mental themes into thoughts that are oriented in the present, ones that create a future that benefit not only you, but the world as well. What if the mind talked about creating your destiny of love by what you are doing in the present? What you are thinking and saying are creating your life, and the world today and tomorrow.

Another purpose of silence is to listen. What do you hear? You are listening for a space of silence like when you are breathing between your inhale and exhale. Focusing on the pause in the breath is a path to enlightenment that Buddha traversed, or so it is said. When you focus on the space of no thought, then you are encountering the space of pure creativity. Within the space of no thought, a new creation emerges, like finding a painting, a novel, or a song.

Thoughts are spontaneously occurring in the mind. You may not be able to stop them, but you do not have to participate with the content. Watch your thoughts float by and notice if you can how your body feels at the mere mention of the brain's idea of a necessary thought. When you allow the thought to dissipate as soon as it appears, then your body will also relax because you are not participating in this creation. Just make a note about the themes of the thoughts because these are the themes that can be running your creations in life, controlling your energetic signature in this space and time. Now you are looking at which came first; the thought or your energy. To change your energy, think new thoughts. Change the way you view the world as if you are seeing it for the first time. Your energy is magnetizing your world into being. Are you ready for a new energy signature?

Love exists within the space between thoughts, between breaths, not love that can cause you pain, but a love that never ends. Most of us never notice this potential, although it is within us all the time. In silence, you may encounter the pure space of creativity and love. You can also encounter a sound current, a humming sound and light, many lines and shapes of light. It is a magical place encountered in meditation, and highly sought as a place of peace, love, and compassion; sometimes known as bliss. We will discuss the space in the breath and meditation in more depth later. For now, just know that silence is your meditation. Remember that meditation is observation.

Silence also gives you an opportunity to heal. Silence is healing to the mind, body, and spirit. Silence within a natural setting can be even more healing because the energy of the Earth is more noticeable when you are not in the middle of a million thinking, chattering people. It is so funny to me when someone tells me that they feel all alone and isolated. I wonder how anyone can feel alone. Aloneness is a complete illusion. You are never alone. When you are silent, you may finally notice that you are not alone. You may find the path out of misery, anger, sadness, and despair. Of course, first, you may have to encounter the demons of your own negative mental chatter. Now, let's get back to our facilitator, and her explanation about the Destiny Retreat.

"We are leaving behind our escape routes of television, conversations, conflict, phones, food, excessive uses of caffeine, alcohol, smoking, drugs, analyzing, arranging, controlling, processing, and being intellectually stimulated. I have probably left out a few of your favorites that will distract you along the way. Your cravings are your cravings for escape. It is the craving of your ego-mind for the instant fix that masquerades as happiness, and it may be the only happiness that you have known. This type of happiness is but a pale reflection of the inner peace that exists deep within each and every one of you.

"THE REALITY YOU HAVE BEEN ESCAPING FROM IS YOU!

"Ask yourself this question: what are you devoted to in this life? In what areas have you been truly committed?

"Then ask yourself this question: where would I be willing to place my devotional energy?

"Here at this retreat, you have an opportunity to observe everything you do and everything you think. And you will miss more than you could ever imagine. You have an opportunity to watch yourself creating your reality. And you will miss yourself creating your reality. This retreat is a pathway, and it is not perfection. You will notice what you are ready to notice, what your intention guides you to notice.

"You have an opportunity to accept where you have been, where you are, and where you are going. The retreat is an opportunity to create your destiny, a life in which you are creating what you feel is worthy of your devotion. When you find that path, the one in your heart that you came to this life to complete, inner peace will arrive. On that day, you will no longer seek, but you will have found love. The love will be within.

"Your destination is inside you. It is an inward journey. You have a challenge to stay silent and become the observer of the ego. SILENCE IS A KEY TO ENLIGHTENMENT. When you are quiet, you can hear the whisper of your inner still small voice, or the roaring thunder of creativity that propels you toward your destiny. Use the key of silence to your advantage.

"You will come to see that the entire purpose of this retreat is to provide you with keys to enlightenment. When you become fully focused on your destiny, you are aware that you are already enlightened, but have been asleep to that awareness. Then, as Mahatma Gandhi said: "Be the change you want to see in the world," and you will become the solution you desire to see. The world will not create a better you. The world will not stop your mind from its games, and in fact, it seems to encourage you to play them forever. Stop looking out at the world for your solutions.

"You are the creator of your destiny. You are the creator of your world. Right now, you may begin creating the destiny that you truly want.

"For the next few days, and for the rest of your life, REMEMBER that the ego-mind will try to interpret everything. The mind belongs to you. It is your tool, and it is like a two-year-old in need of boundaries and focus. And, like a two-year-old, your brain may kick and scream when you set a limit because you have been buying it a toy every time you shop, for too long. It is your choice whether you allow its decisions to influence your reality simply by your past. Open your mind, your vision, and truly observe the world and your reactions. Focus on your destiny and maintain the focus. Then, your two-year-old will smile and enjoy the peace, love, and compassion that is like spending a quiet day building a castle in the sand at the ocean.

"To help you observe more efficiently, you are being given

personal journals to keep. While you are here, constantly listen to, and observe your mind talking and look upon it as chatter. Record this chatter that we will label mind talk. In your journals, use the journal questions and backs of the pages to record your mind talk. Notice that your mind talk will have running themes. What are these themes? While recording these themes, notice which ones may be themes that have run through your mind for a lifetime? How long have some of these themes been with you? For example, your mind might have a running theme of, "Never being good enough." Do you have to participate with this? Do you have to let it ruin your day and be your opinion of who you are? ABSOLUTELY NOT! Will you be tempted to participate? ABSOLUTELY YES!

"What happens when you can choose to stay out of participation with a running theme of the mind, one that has been running your life? A MIRACLE! Your vision will expand to encompass possibilities you may never have thought imaginable. In the example above, you might think for once that you are not only good enough, but maybe you are lovable. You can expect an argument; the kicking and screaming of the mind to be loud. Stay consistent in your determination to move your consciousness to a loving topic, the creation of your destiny.

"The back of your journal pages can also be used to note any coincidences that may occur while you are here, or while you were planning to attend. So-called coincidences occur all the time. One coincidence you might notice right away would be any similarities you have with your fellow participants, or others you encounter. Many times, you fail to notice these coincidences or just dismiss them. Perhaps this is due to the fact that you are also failing to appreciate the miraculous qualities all around you. You are noisy, busy, and distracted, but once you are in this observational state, you will begin to notice that the universe is talking. You will notice that one of the extraordinary results of quieting your mind will be more and more coincidences that begin to guide you through your life experiences. By the time you reach the third day, perhaps you will be fully hearing the universe around you.

"Write about everything your mind fabricates about this reality that you are creating. The journal is only for you, no one else. Reread your journal in order to utilize its full benefits.

"Remember to always thank your mind for its input. The mind is trying to sort through all the sensory material that you encounter. The ego-mind is trying to protect you by staying in its survival mode. Realize the whole truth is not the ego-mind's interpretation of events. A much greater truth lies outside of your thoughts, just beyond your conscious awareness. The ego is stuck in the past. The ego is stuck in fear, and is obsessed with survival. To move from fear to love, one must release fear and find trust. You are here to relax and be in love. You are here to be in the moment, and to be present. Be the observer! Observe everything. You are here to be conscious. Be conscious of everything you think, of your entire internal world. Be conscious of everything your senses scan, your entire external world.

"Starting right now, do everything consciously! Be aware of everything you are doing. Be conscious of your eating, conscious of your breathing, conscious of your mind chatter, and conscious of your body movement. Be totally aware of your environment. Be totally aware of your judgments, and write about them. How many times in your life have you used the same judgments over and over again? Having judgments about others is ALWAYS about judgments you have against yourself. Always! Writing these judgments in your journal will help you to reach acceptance of yourself and of others. ACCEPTANCE IS ANOTHER KEY TO ENLIGHTENMENT. You move into judgment in order to escape. It is the same kind of distraction as eating, drinking, or smoking would be. When you start to observe how you move through life unaware of how these judgments create negative realities, it will help you to move into awareness of other areas of your life.

"Quiet your voice and listen. Stop your activities and listen. Finally, still your mind and listen. Get conscious. Listen to your thoughts, and your thoughts about others. As you do this, you will pick up on the thoughts and the energy of others. You will find out that you really do not need words to communicate. You receive communication in other ways. You receive energy in other ways. Listen in the other ways. LISTEN. LISTENING IS A KEY TO ENLIGHTENMENT.

"When you are in a group, notice your thoughts. They are not always your thoughts. You will pick up on the thoughts of whoever is around you. In a large group, you may pick up the consensus of whatever the group thoughts may be. This group consciousness will often be lead by the individuals who are sending out the strongest thoughts. We were born with the power to tune into energy. When you walk into a room with a baby, the baby will immediately pick up on your energy. Have you ever seen an infant who starts crying when someone agitated walks into the room? A newborn knows if a person is stressed out, frustrated, or angry, and will reflect this in their behavior. If you had this power as a baby, you still have it now. You may have simply forgotten how to use this. Or your big talkative brain is now busy falsely labeling the energy you feel.

"What are you using this power for now?

"To what channel are you tuned?

"What energy are you most likely to notice?

"What does your mind talk to you about all the time?

"What kind of energy do you work and live around, and how is it affecting your life and your destiny?

"As we grew up, the mind learned to make up stories about how you were feeling. It fantasizes that it knows everything that is happening. It makes up reality the way it wants to see it, and tells you that this is the truth. It is constantly interpreting events as it sees fit. Stop and question the mind's assumptions. Whenever your mind tells you what someone else is thinking, or what someone else's motivation is, YOU ARE WRONG. When you realize your mind is doing this, STOP, and question its assumptions. STOP, and write about your mind talk at the moment you catch yourself mind reading. NO ONE IS A MIND READER. You are an energy sensor. Talk about the energy, thus eliminating the fiction from the story.

"Remember to journal often. The journal assignments are for you to help find yourself. The journal is to help you realize that you will be much happier living in acceptance of yourself and others. Do not look at the journals as something that has to be done correctly.

"You made the decision to be here. You made the decision to find out about yourself. You made the decision that there was something of value here. We are here to show you the best techniques that we know. Writing in the journal is one of the most effective tools we have found in becoming aware of what thought systems are running your mind. This is a tool that works. It is not enough to simply read the question and say, 'I have read the questions, but I only need to read them. I will just think about this and it will be enough.'

"Please give the journal writing exercises your full attention, and write the answers. You may surprise yourself. Let go and write freely without editing your answers. These answers are for your eyes only.

"Remember, if you think you need to speak, stop and write about the need to speak, and write about what you want to say. What is your goal, your motivation for speaking? Understand that whenever you think you need to speak, you may have a hidden agenda for this need. What could it be?

"And now, stay silent, stay conscious, and observe as much as you possibly can. You will never see it all at once. Life is a process. As you become aware, life unfolds and consciousness continues to expand. Remember, you are here to become your destiny, to find your way home."

Chapter Three Journal Questions

1. Write about your worries. Put them in a list according to their importance.
2. Look at your number one worry. How old is this worry?
3. How did your worry originate? Do you know when and how you first decided to have this worry?
4. Who were your worry examples in life? (Hint: Could you feel some compassion for your role models when you realize they had this kind of suffering too?)
5. Write about the solution for your problem. What steps would it take to be rid of it?
6. Write about how it feels to be rid of the worry.
7. If you don't worry, write about the topics on which your mind dwells. What is your mind saying to you?
8. After you solve one problem, the second one will appear? Write about how it feels to see this process.
9. How do you feel about silence?
10. What do you hear when you silence the mind for a moment?
11. How does your mind or your distractions keep you from expanding your consciousness?

Chapter 4 Looking Yourself in the Eye

"The meeting of two personalities is like the contact of two chemical substances; if there is any reaction, both are transformed."
–Carl Jung (1875 – 1961)

"You cannot depend on your eyes when your imagination is out of focus."
–Mark Twain (1835 - 1910), From A Connecticut Yankee in King Arthur's Court

Reality is a world of reflections; a mirror of your beliefs. All of creation is composed of a sea of energy of which you are a connected speck. Have you ever wondered why some parts of the energetic soup appear to be drawn in your direction, while other bits of energy appear to be repelled? Or why, for a moment in time, you are next to someone and the next moment you are unable to make any connection whatsoever? Is the energy chaotically moving around with no directional guidance system, or is it somehow being attracted and repelled by your intention? If you entertain the possibility that you are influencing (maybe not controlling) the interactions you are having with energy, then you will begin to understand how you are creating and not creating your life.

Now, let's look at a literal demonstration of how this reality forms around the beliefs of our participants in their next activity.

'Oh no, we are going to what? Do a process to determine our

roommates? What the hell is a process in these people's demented minds, and I definitely do not want to even think about that person across from me. I am planning to spend my weekend with Janna, and to keep that woman over there as far away from my room and space as possible. Oh well, the music is very beautiful, and this place is peaceful. If only I could just relax and we would stop doing things that make me uncomfortable.' Melanie is not only judging her reality here, but she is creating a reality right now! She is influencing energy, placing forth an energetic signal to the woman across from her, spewing energy in many directions. Others are actually sensing something from her as well.

Once again, the facilitator in the front of the room tells the group to get comfortable and relax. Rather than relaxing music, for the first time some rather uncomfortable music begins to play. It is almost agitating in a way. The music matches the unsettled feelings in the room. The facilitator's insistent voice gives directions about noticing thoughts and feelings.

"Close your eyes. Take a deep breath. Right now, we are going to be selecting partners. Think about the people in the room. Think about how you feel about them. Who did you notice? How many people do you think you dismissed from your attention? Who do you like, and who do you dislike. What is your mind telling you about the others in this room?"

This activity seems to go on and on until finally everyone has a partner and it culminates as everyone is divided into groups of two or three. These people will become partners for most of the retreat. The significance of the selection of partners in the seminar symbolizes your ability to draw and repel people in your daily life. It symbolizes how you influence energy. In other words, this creation of a partner can help you see how you create your own reality.

Relationships are an adventure, and right now that adventure begins again as you look around and notice consciously who you have attracted, repelled, and ignored in your life. Wherever you go, you are confronted with people. Unless you are a hermit living in a cave with no television, no cell phone, and no contact, you will have people constantly surrounding you. Others are everywhere, and your mind is evaluating all the people you notice. Even when you think that you are in isolation, you are connected to the energy of the rest of the world. If you are unaware of your connection to that energy, which is often the case, then you are simply asleep to the energy in your environment. It still exists, and you are very aware on a subconscious level.

To make matters more complicated, your mind is dismissing huge portions of your environment. How does your mind decide who to notice and who not to notice? Again, it is very important to observe yourself. Watch who and what you are noticing. Observe what you are not observing. Pay close attention to what kinds of statements the mind is making as you begin to see the magnitude of this process more fully. How does that mind talk affect your mood, your emotions, and feelings? Notice any accompanying physical sensations.

Is may feel odd to observe yourself observing others? Even more ridiculous is to observe yourself ignoring much of your surroundings. Once you observe all the people you have previously ignored, you are now observing yourself observing them. This observational process is a key to enlightenment, especially when you become aware of how you are thinking, feeling, the mood you have, your emotions, and your physical sensations. It is especially important to closely observe events in which you have intense emotional reactions. These kinds of reactions actually keep you even more distracted from the rest of the world in general. If you expand your view in this way during intense emotional reactions, you will find that you may have a slow motion feeling, like walking through molasses. You are in an issue, distracted by one event, and unable to attend to simple activities that usually require little energy to accomplish. Imagine that you are looking at an ocean and all you see is one drop of water, and that one drop is triggering a huge emotional response, so huge that the ocean disappears and only that drop appears.

As you practice expanding your view, you could first observe that you don't have any energy about many people in the world, having ignored certain people for a lifetime. Your absence of thought about someone could be about a clerk in a grocery store two aisles over. Or it could be the people comprising a crowd at an event. For instance, how many individual people do you notice at an airport? If you are one of those people who like to people-watch, then watch what your mind is saying to you about those attention-catching individuals, and continue to look around, and observe the rest of humanity more closely.

The mind is limited by how much information it can cope with. You learn from childhood to process out large quantities of information about others. In a big group, the mind often scans the room for threat, and in finding none, dismisses the problem. Of course, this tactic will not keep you safe in the event that a crowd becomes threatening once you have dismissed a threat. Becoming aware of the energy of the crowd is how you become safer.

I am not suggesting that you become agitated by crowds, although many are. Crowds invigorate others. If you are someone that is agitated, it may be because you cannot process all that information/energy and enjoy what you came to enjoy at the same time. At least, you cannot at this time. You may be more empathic than others, taking in the feelings around you as if you are wide open. There are ways to protect yourself. Once you learn to relax your body, read energy, and observe while not participating, you can go anywhere you want to go without discomfort. Relaxation, which we will discuss in more detail later, can set you free of debilitating anxiety.

For now, begin to notice how much you don't notice about others. Pay attention to all the people you scan and dismiss. Closely observe the sales clerks, and fellow travelers on your planet. Observe again, and notice how unthreatening they appear to be to your brain. If you keep observing, it can become very obvious to you that the mind is often focused on that which gives it discomfort, or that which gives it distraction. In other words, every person on the planet is uniquely paying attention to certain people.

When I go out to lunch with my business partner, being therapists we are keenly aware of dysfunctional behavior that is happening all around us. It is both a curse and a blessing. But I will notice one type of person and she will notice another. We are focused in two different directions. Being more observational than most people, I also notice the disparity between our two unique focuses, her emotion, my emotion, and our obvious lack of emotion toward everything else. I am also practicing relaxation and meditating. This focus is called multidimensional awareness, and appears to be a seemingly unlimited concept with which the mind struggles to grasp, and in fact is accomplished with much more ease when completely relaxed, releasing the need for control.

Everyone's mind varies on how it processes the surrounding flow of humanity. Some people are socially phobic, very anxious about others to the point of refusing to leave the safety of the house. They fear the world, and avoid being around a few strangers. The mind runs amok in this case, making up dangerous fantasies about those who are safe, or projecting that others are negatively judging them in the same way. Fear of losing control also accompanies these awful scenarios, creating avoidance of new situations. In other words, the mind is thinking that everyone else thinks like it does. Wrong! Others do not think like you do. If another person is being that negative, then they are afraid of you!

Then, you have the extroverts who become energized by a crowd. They are so stimulated by crowds that they can be crushed in a stampede at an event. They are in the middle of the action, trying to get as much from the crowd as possible. The mind has decided in this case that the crowd is fun. By the way, the extrovert cannot believe that others do not think like their mind either! That is why an extrovert just cannot believe that an introvert wouldn't have tons of fun once they leave the confines of their isolation.

But can you believe it, an introvert, someone who isn't energized by the group, can be crushed in a stampede, and perhaps even more easily than the extrovert? The mind decides what information to filter, and what to address. If your mind does not address the explosiveness of a crowd as dangerous when it is, then you can be trampled. If your mind is busy thinking about every little detail, you can forget about the big picture, the simple explanation for how society functions most of the time. A friend of mine is always saying to me, "Don't be a lemming."

Once again, the mind decides who to notice and who to ignore. This process creates your personal reality. You think that your reality is based on facts. But what you are calling facts is only the limited amount of reality that you are observing at the moment. The rest of the world is vague, and resting beyond your awareness. Many of your facts are lies that your mind tells you about the actions of others.

What or who comes to the forefront of your awareness is an individual decision based on your survival system, inherited by your genetic code, and reinforced by the experiences you have had in your family of origin.

What does all of this information all mean? It means, for example, if your mother or father were not to be trusted, that your mind is waiting to prove that all women or men cannot be trusted. Your mind is waiting, watching, and interpreting men or women with the predetermined notion that they are not to be trusted. What is worse is that alongside this preconceived notion lurks a mind hooked on a chaotic activity, like being addicted to smoking. It is addicted to looking for untrustworthy men or women. And to make matters even worse, you could be falling in love with a truly untrustworthy person, and spend your life trying to make him or her more trustworthy! You could be trying to fix individuals, including your children, who were actually trustworthy to begin with.

Imagine getting in a relationship with someone who cannot be trusted, and then trying to make them become trustworthy! You have my sincere good wishes for good health insurance so that you can afford to go to therapy and maybe the doctor as well. Fixing or rescuing people can create an illness in your body. You are not designed to handle emotions other than your own, and even these are often intolerable. I have many years of experience making myself ill trying to fix others. It really is true that you cannot change another person just because you need them to change. The only way a person changes is if they want to change, and even then they may fail. If they succeed, they most likely could have many relapses along the way.

Your beliefs instill in you the tendency to draw people into your life who will match your original opinions. Even if, by some lucky chance, they don't match your beliefs, you can still warp your reality to make them match.

For example, let's say that you have the belief that women are untrustworthy. You have a relationship with a woman, either

Looking Yourself in the Eye

as a friend or lover. She says that she will get off work at 5:00 PM but leaves her work at 5:30 PM. You could feel totally betrayed and convinced that she cannot be trusted.

But to make matters worse, you will possibly draw women into your life who will never keep their word. In this way, you will never change your belief. It will be like you are a magnet for untrustworthy women. You have a 'women are not to be trusted' filter over your mind, and your mind only notices disappointment.

This reality is a paradox. You won't be able to notice women who are trustworthy, so for all intents and purposes, they don't exist for you. You may always draw untrustworthy women into your life, which constantly reinforces your belief that women cannot be trusted. By the way, you will also pay attention to them in restaurants. How will you be able notice how profoundly your beliefs are helping to create the problem? The answer would be to learn to observe.

Do you have a belief about others that you can identify? Everyone has strong beliefs about others. Strong beliefs are those that crowd out reality, and bring forth a rush of intense emotional energy. These beliefs define men, women, children, religion, politics, how others should or should not be treated, and so on. They are the beliefs that cause a conflict at the dinner table, at work, and ultimately create war. Your beliefs are determining your reality by directing your focus. How could you really cure a belief about untrustworthy women if you had one? You would have to be able to notice all the women who are trustworthy, and continue believing in their existence even though your mind wants to continually find lack of trust.

It sounds a little difficult, doesn't it? Like any new skill, it takes some practice to move your mind from its beliefs to other possible realities.

Of course, the opposite situation also occurs. Let's say that you trust men implicitly. You attract very trustworthy men. Do you notice that many are untrustworthy? Yes, you may have that experience on the periphery of your reality, and you may be puzzled by it. After all, extremely untrustworthy people often grab the headlines. You may think that you just have great luck because you never have men like that in your life. In fact, it seems as if you live on another plane of existence, and, in fact, you do.

Think about the people in your life. Who are your associates? Imagine that you are in a room filled with 100 people. Who is attracting your attention? Who do you usually find in a crowd? Are you looking for someone in particular? Do you usually find that person in the room? If you find the person, what does your mind fear about the person? How will your mind create its problem with the person; even bringing it out of them so it can obsess on the problem? The obsession part is the part that is triggered with emotion, the part that takes over. When you become one with the belief and the intense emotion, the mind will begin to think about it over and over. At that point, you lose your ability to observe, and you become the problem, the thoughts, and the emotions. In fact, you may lose your ability to observe your surroundings the minute you spot your so-called problem.

It is very mystical that in a room full of people, you can find the one who reflects your beliefs, and even more intense, you could get in a relationship with that one special person you find attractive across a world full of people. You are repelled and attracted at the same time. You are locked into the magnet of your belief.

Think about all the people you are presently noticing in your life. Think about the issues that you have had in your life with others. In a room full of 100 people, you can easily find that issue. Observation of all the people you generally ignore in that room will open your reality to new potential outcomes. About 99 of those people will not be your issue. When you have learned your lesson from your issue, you could associate with one of the unnoticed ones.

Life is like a house of mirrors. Everyone you become aware of is reflecting your belief in you in an almost magical process. It is a mystery that in a room full of people when randomly selected, a person will be paired with others who have significant coincidental lessons for each other. We prove it over and over and over, when we put strangers together for a weekend seminar. It should not be such a mystery to us that our minds are so linked together. How have we come to ignore our connection? We all have beliefs that create our view of reality.

The person that you dislike the most is the greatest mirror that you will encounter. Remember that you are their magnet, and if you do not like that reflection, then the change begins within you. What is the message in the mirror? Learn it and it won't keep appearing. Refuse to go there and the mirror will keep reflecting the same image over and over, until you understand it, forgive it, and love it.

Now, let's get back to our participants. Melanie is not too happy with her partner. She is agonizing over her concerns as she meets with her new partner for the retreat. They are not talking, only looking at each other as directed by the same facilitator that started this process. Music is playing, suggesting a direction to take with this situation. Melanie is not able to hear the words of music consciously, because her mind is deafening.

'I just cannot believe I have this problem. I came here to find peace of mind and now I am in a room all weekend with someone I cannot stand. How will I ever really relax with this woman in my space all of the time? I could sort of ignore her, maybe go off by myself, or forget to wait for her. I could just find Janna and spend some quality time with her, but what if...

What if I get caught? God, I am beginning to sound like a fourteen-year-old. What is wrong with me? I just wanted to learn some relaxation and find some meaning in my life. This problem may keep me from finding the meaning I want so desperately to find. Maybe they will change our partners tomorrow. Yeah, maybe we won't really have to stay like this.' Melanie is obsessing again about her big problem in life at the moment. This big problem is even going to be the so-called reason that she can't move forward for the whole weekend if her mind has its way.

'I just cannot believe I am going to spend any time with this woman! How can this happen, that I am with the only person in the room I cannot stand? Perhaps I will be able to connect with some of the other people here. Wow! I am exhausted. I wonder how much longer this will go on tonight.

'Well, at least I won't have any problem conversing with Deanna since we cannot talk. At least I don't have to make nice conversation with her when we are in our room. Yes, I think I can be the most silent person here!' Melanie is quite relieved to have an escape method of silence practically handed to her on a silver platter. She is also feeling very smug about her ability to complete this task of silence now that she has a buddy she cannot stomach.

Deanna is feeling more nervous than ever. 'Why did I think I could live without cigarettes for a weekend? I better find my nicotine gum. How the hell can I survive being alone with my mind for hours, much less two days? I may go crazy. That woman Melanie looks positively happy about this turn of events. What is wrong with her anyway? She is a cold one. I think I had better talk to one of those facilitators and see what they suggest to help me cope with this, since I obviously can't stand this silence.'

Look at Melanie's reaction to her roommate, Deanna. She

has never spoken to the woman and yet has instantaneous negative reactions based on equally quick judgments she makes in her head every time she sees or hears Deanna. Her feelings are so intense that she is devising escape plans, engaging in wishful thinking about being moved to a new roommate situation, and deciding that this lone woman can be the cause of failure for her whole weekend. You see, Deanna triggers a memory of something else beneath her consciousness. She has no conscious awareness of the connection. Yes, she is having an intense emotional reaction to an innocuous situation, and feels a need to escape. Her need is not so intense to make her leave, but intense enough to plan the rejection of another person.

Isn't it interesting that she finds herself with the addict, a master of escape, who is also looking for ways to escape Melanie's coldhearted energy? With Deanna, the primary one she needs to escape is her own relentless negative mind.

Once again, the facilitator interrupts Melanie's thoughts with instructions. She says, "Answer the next two journal questions." Thankfully, Melanie can record some of the thoughts she is having, but is hesitant to say too many bad things about her partner for fear Deanna might just see what she has written. She sighs and begins writing, as music softly plays in the background.

Throughout the retreat, the participants are asked to answer questions in their journals, with music quietly playing in the background.

Find some motivating music and answer your own journal questions below, and remember to record your mind talk about this information.

Chapter 4 Journal Questions

1. What are some of your beliefs about men? (Hint: begin with your family of origin.)
2. What are some of your beliefs about women? (Same hint!)
3. What types of men and women do you attract into your life?
4. What types of problems do you have with others in general?
5. Who do you wish that you could have in your life, and for what purpose?
6. Who do wish you could avoid, and who do you dislike?
7. Who are you ignoring? (To answer this question may take some time to observe who you have placed on mute.)
8. What do you think that people are reflecting to you in your world?

Chapter 5 State Your Intentions

"Before you agree to do anything that might add even the smallest amount of stress to your life, ask yourself: What is my truest intention? Give yourself time to let a yes resound within you. When it's right, I guarantee that your entire body will feel it."

–Oprah Winfrey (1954-)

"Before we set our hearts too much upon anything, let us examine how happy those are who already possess it."

–Francois de La Rochefoucauld (1613 - 1680)

The facilitator begins a new activity after the end of the journal writing. She continually patiently waits until everyone is almost finished with their writing before beginning each new round of instructions. "Right now, you will have another opportunity to decide what you are going to create this weekend. Sit for a moment in silence and listen to yourself, to your inner self and ask, 'What is my intention this weekend?' Allow an answer to form and then take your journal and permit yourself to write anything that comes forth, without editing or judging the result. If your mind makes judgments or comments about your intention, write those statements as well."

As the participants are listening to their inner voice for an intention, you can stop reading for a moment and do the same assignment. It is journal question number one at the end of this chapter. What is your intention? You also can read the full discussion of intentions before you write it. Or you have the option of listening to yourself right now, and then doing it again at the end of this chapter to see if you hear the same intention again.

You set an intention based on that question we were talking about before: "To what do you wish to be devoted?" What are you trying to create in your life, or what would you like to create? An intention could be to have a better relationship with your husband, or it could be to work toward world peace. Wouldn't those be almost the same intentions since you will never have world peace if you cannot be at peace with yourself and your family? When the participants first wrote a statement about why they wanted to attend this retreat, they set an intention. When they introduced themselves and said why they were here, they set an intention. When you picked up this book, you had a desire in mind. But have the participants, and have you ever just stopped for a second to really listen to what intention you want to set for your life right now? Is it true that the road to hell is paved with good intentions? The road to hell is actually paved with wishes that sound like intentions, but have never contained any devotion.

Oh, the mind might say something survival motivated like, "I intend to make a million dollars," and that would be an intention. Look again and again at what your purpose is for setting your intention. Will that intention finally fix your life and make you happy? Back up a minute then. Beware of intentions that have those 'fix-it' qualities to them.

Exactly how can a person set a really good intention, one that is not based on survival, fear, lack, and ego-based desires? Plus, we don't want to set an intention just because we think we should want something, like for instance world peace, if it is a superficial wish, one to which we would not devote ourselves. In other words, saying the words is easy. The crux of the solution is to ask yourself if you are willing to take action, or are you really devoted to this intention?

Now, I am not suggesting that you need to know how you are going to fulfill any intentions you are setting, because often you will not know how until you actually have the goal firmly in mind. The how is created by the goal, not the other way around. It's like finding a parking place in an overcrowded parking lot. When your mind says that there are no parking places, then your mind cannot see a parking place. When you set an intention that a parking place really can exist, even though you have not seen it yet, then almost magically, the parking angel provides you with a parking place in front. Theories suggest that the mind cannot see what it does not believe. Think about why drivers pull out in front of motorcycles. Is it because they were only looking for cars and did not see the motorcycle or pedestrian, or other moving objects?

Our realities are limited by our beliefs.

When you stop thinking that you know what you want to make you happy, and instead, listen to what direction to take, what goal is whispering quietly inside you, then you have a great intention. You have roadmap in your heart if you will only be very quiet, and listen.

But don't worry. You can start with an intention of making a million dollars, and you will still get to the intention that really burns in your soul. Why would that be? It is said that all paths lead to God. How would I know it is true? I can only say that I observe the oddest of paths lead to God. It seems that the universe will spare no expense in showing us the truth. Factually, some paths take a longer route than others. My personal theory, not unique to me I am sure, is that if one wants the quicker, less painful path, then stay focused on God so God doesn't have to take any sledgehammers to get your attention. Take the heart path.

The question of intention wouldn't be what my mind thinks is a good idea because that would be ego-based, survival motivated perhaps. The intention question would be what God wants to express through me on this planet.

Now, what if you don't believe in God? Are you in the wrong book? But seriously, do you believe you are totally isolated and alone, disconnected from the rest of universe and nothing you do affects others? If you think of you in connection with the whole of the universe, and that the universe is completely intelligent, then what intention would that universe want to manifest through you? Now you have a magnificent intention. However, if you manifest becoming pregnant, married in a perfect relationship, making more money, etc, you will be getting closer, because you are moving toward a relationship with the universe that wants to give you everything.

The way I visualize a human is like an empty receptacle that the universe wants to fill if only the lid is removed. However, I do think we have a lid on top, and our job is to slowly open that lid more and more and more. Some people open it really wide and then slam it closed, as in make a million, lose a million. Some people open it a little way and feel very comfortable, so they try to hold it right there in a little safe rut. The lid will slowly edge back toward closed when you try that one. It seems like the universe is expanding, and as such, it seems to work really well if we keep opening more and more. Oh sure, sometimes you have to hold still to adjust to the new openness for a while, but if you try to stay the same, you seem to close up again. Keep opening, like a flower eternally blooming on this planet, until you take your last breath. After that moment, who knows? All I can say is that I imagine the death of a fully blooming flower as something much better than a bud that died on the vine because it was afraid to open. And then, maybe there is always reincarnation where we eternally have another chance to bloom, to become fearless.

With your intention, will you be willing to exercise devotion? An intention alone will just sit there and be annoying, filling you with guilt. The reason you do not have this intention manifested yet is because you are blocked, of course. Anything you want is a lie. You do not want it, you fear it. Anything you say you want, you really do not want. If you didn't fear it, you would already have it. Look at people who say they want a relationship. That means you don't have one. WANT means LACK. Here is your paradox that you will be observing in silence and meditation as you look at creating your destiny. You create the manifestation of your intention by giving up lack.

Set an intention and then you can observe how it affects you, and how you are blocked from your devotion to it, how you create lack. Although it sounds insidious, really you can give up lack quite easily. I didn't say painlessly because sometimes you like to suffer to give up lack. However, the suffering is an illusion.

Let's look at our participants and see how they are doing with their third chance at finding an intention.

Melanie is feeling so tight that she has a migraine headache at the edge of her consciousness. 'A baby is my intention? Oh come on, I cannot believe that the only thing I hear when I close my eyes and listen to my heart is baby. My head is starting to hurt. Baby! Shouldn't my intention be some important life purpose or something? I don't get it! I do want to have a baby and have for some time but... I don't think I am ready. I am not ready financially and I am too nervous. What kind of mother could I be when I am this nervous, and look at this headache just thinking about it. If this was right, I would feel good, not bad. Why can't I just come up with something that sounds more important and easier?'

Deanna is totally surprised. She thought her intention would be to work more on her sobriety. Instead, she is hearing that she wants to become a counselor like the people who have helped her in her life. 'I can't do that. I am not smart enough. I am too old. I would never be able to go through everything it takes. Look how long it would take? I would be forty years old by the time I got out of school. Who starts being a counselor when they are forty? It takes too long! Wow! I just think I better set an intention to go to the gym more often, because I need to look a lot better and get more endorphins. Look how fat I look next to Melanie. She is so tiny and cute. I need to work out every day. I can't even get myself to the gym to look better. How could I possibly have the discipline to go to school for years?'

Sophie had set an intention to spend more quality time with Madison, so she is actually enjoying the fact that she is now living a destiny right now that she created last time she came to the retreat. She is lovingly watching her daughter, who is furiously writing away about her goals in life.

Madison knows exactly what she wants in life. She has been a lazy student but she loves to read. She writes beautifully, and dreams of being able to write books one day like the ones she loves to read. And like many young girls, she envisions herself in a perfect relationship some day, with a couple of equally perfect children in a perfect home. Madison wants the American Dream. When she looks at the couple in the room, she adds that she wants the kind of relationship that can really do things like this together too!

So let's talk about the intentions that are floating around a bit. Melanie and Deanna are so perfect for each other. They are both instantly intuitive, hearing a beautiful intention and then smashing it with their lethal minds. Deanna went a step further and planned an intention that many will try, the infamous 'gym to look better' intention.

Why is the gym a problem? It would be a great place to get

healthier, theoretically, and give her the endorphins she could use, except her motivation is all wrong. She is going because she hates herself. The reason people both buy a membership and fail to go, or buy a membership and go excessively is because of self-hate. Moderation at the gym arrives with self-love. No self-love existed in this intention.

Madison is an overachieving, idealistic youth, with a great plan, and she is also in touch with her inner love; writing books. She even includes the potential of having it all. Pray she keeps her optimism.

Now, how are you feeling about your intention? A great intention is something that has some self-love within it. It is something that resonates in your soul and not something that is going to fix your life, or make you look good enough. A good intention is something that even if it takes time, you will be doing what you want to do, and the time will be well spent. See Deanna complaining about the pain of time, when she forgets that she loves to do that type of learning! So what if it took the rest of her life? She would be doing what she yearns to do. So what if Melanie had that baby while she was still not perfect. The baby could motivate her to be a good mother. And of course, maybe a baby would teach her how to love herself.

Are you seeing that it might be a good idea to look really closely at the goal that your soul yearns for, while observing your excuses as something battling your soul's desire? Hello! Your soul has an intention. Listen. Your brain may be sabotaging your soul's intentions.

Chapter 5 Journal Questions

1. What is your intention? (Hint: write the first intention you hear inside.)
2. What is your mind saying to you about your intention?

3. If you have more than one intention, look at them and see if you can find a link between them. (Hint: the link usually comes from your childhood.)
4. Write about how much you do NOT want to manifest this intention. Pretend to be negative if you have to. Record how you feel, especially pay attention to feelings, thoughts, and body sensations. Notice the fear.
5. Write about how much you want to manifest this intention. Again, pay attention to your thoughts, emotions and body sensations. Notice the fear/excitement, which are very closely related.
6. What is your intention now?

Chapter 6 Remember Love

> *"Grandfather,*
> *Sacred One,*
> *Teach us love, compassion, and honor,*
> *That we may heal the earth*
> *And heal each other."*
>
> –Ojibway prayer

> *"Man is his own star and the soul that can render an honest and perfect man commands all light, all influence, all fate."*
>
> –John Fletcher (1579 – 1625)

"Get comfortable." This time a man is speaking.

'I wish I could remember their names. Who are these people, these facilitators? Sometimes, they seem so serene, and sometimes, they feel almost agitated. I wonder how they got into this retreat business.' Melanie is feeling very tired and losing her focus rapidly. 'I cannot believe this woman (Deanna) is sitting right next to me all the time now!' Melanie begins to fluff her pillow and pulls her blanket up around her chin. She is feeling sort of weird and tense. 'I don't feel very relaxed! Janna looks so peaceful! What I would give to look that happy!'

Deanna is actually falling asleep before her head hits her pillow. The last thought drifts by as the music starts, 'How can I keep falling asleep in a room full of people when I usually have insomnia?'

The lights dim and beautiful music is playing once more.

REMEMBER LOVE

(©Diane Donovan-Vaughn, 1996 words by David Donovan & Diane Donovan-Vaughn)

"Close your eyes and take several deep breaths. Feel the breath flow naturally in and out. Just relax and fill your lungs with fresh clean air. Feel your whole body thriving on and responding to this fresh supply of air. Feel your whole body, every cell, being at peace from this focus on pure breath. Picture a pillar of brilliant white light coming down from as far out in the universe as your mind can imagine. It is warm and comforting. It is the ultimate representation of pure love and acceptance.

"The light travels time and space to be with you. Your simple thought of wishing it to be there is all it takes to bring this light to you. The light comes from far beyond, with a brilliant radiance flowing through you. See this pillar coming down around you and surrounding your entire body. Your entire being is filled with this light. Allow this pillar of light to flow through your feet and enter the earth. The pillar of light then flows to the very core of the earth itself. See the flow of pure love and light flowing into you from the universe, then flowing down through you and down into the center of the earth, as a wonderful union. The earth, the universe, and you are all one at this point in time.

"This pillar of light and love is always there for you and always will be. This point in time is now like all others. Your pure-hearted desire, your wish for it to be so, creates this beautiful experience. You know that this is the truth. Just hold the thought in your mind, and at any time you can be one with

this universal source of light and pure love.

"Let's create a story. It isn't fiction or non-fiction. It is just a story. It begins before you came to this life. You are in a place that is brilliant and white and pure. You can see yourself as a perfected form of brilliant spirit, of pure being. You are in a place that is the very essence of that pillar of white light you have around you right now. You are in a place that is so large that it appears to go on forever, without end.

"Everywhere in this place, the white light is around everything you encounter. See this place in your mind. Picture it exactly as you want it to be. Feel the peace of this place.

"You may see large structures that seem to climb forever into the sky. You may notice forests, rivers, mountains, and oceans. It is a place of peace and tranquility. Listen closely and you will hear soft music that seems to be in harmony with everything here. This is a place you have been many times before now. This is the place that you call home. You have an infinite family here, many friends, and teachers. What do you call these people who are your group here? Look around and allow yourself to find a personal guide among these people, who can help you while you are here. Your life here goes on for much more time than you can imagine. It is timeless. The people you are with have been with you since the beginning of time as you know it. It is here that you have the knowledge that time is just an illusion.

"It is here that you can feel that your true purpose is to know love. Your purpose is to learn and grow. You wish to develop. You want to learn all the lessons possible for you. While you are here, you understand that all of your lessons are learned with pure love. In this place of light and love, you have the power to learn everything.

"You know that you can stay right here, in this place, forever. You also know that you have many choices. One of those

choices that you have is to leave this place. 'But why,' you ask yourself, 'would I ever want to leave a place of such unconditional love and acceptance? Why would I want to leave my home?'

"And from deep within you, the answer comes. You realize that the choice to leave is a gift; a gift created by the font of light and love. It is a wonderful gift called life. You have the choice to leave your home and embark on a beautiful adventure called human life. The reason you would accept such a gift is because it is a challenge. It is a perfect way for you to advance as a spirit. You may grow through lessons of such magnitude that can best be learned here on Earth. Earth by her very nature is here to be a profound school. With this knowledge and knowing the gift of life had come from the source of light and love, you accept life.

"With this goal in mind, sit down with your guide and discuss all the possibilities for your human life. You are able to go to a special viewing about your upcoming life, and you are given many options of lives that you might live. You and your guide both know what will be the best life for you. You both know which life will teach you the lessons you need at this stage in your development.

"Now, go to a central meeting place. Here, you meet with many of the people who will be significant to you in your life. Many of these people are from your own group. You also meet with different choices for your parents. All of these people are those who can learn as much from you in this life as you can learn from them. Have discussions with everyone you can. Intricately put your whole life plan together. Assemble life lessons together that will cater to your advancement in this life. Of all the many choices you have, you finally make your decisions. Make your choices and start the plan in motion. Know that you have picked the perfect life, from all of your many options. The life you choose is the one you are now in. It is this *life!*

"You know that you will not come to Earth with any of the knowledge that you have in this place. To have this knowledge in life will not be helpful to your learning, and so you agree. You know that part of the challenge of human life will be to remember the lessons that you need to create. Remember your search for advancement. You know this can be difficult, but you are given tools to aid you in this challenge. You and your group are able to set up sign posts to help you each remember one another. The greatest tasks that you can do in human life are to live the path that you choose for yourself and to find your group.

"Set up signals to help you remember your group. These have to be very simple signals so that you can remember. If they are too complicated, you might mistake these signs for something else. They are little things, and yet not so little. They might be a certain look, the way someone walks, a flash of recognition behind their eyes the first time you meet them.

These recognition signs can be as simple as a feeling of being in that place or with that person before, even though you know in this life that you never have. There is a very important key to remembering your path when you see one of these signs. Remember the purest state of love that you can. Stay in love. If all else seems not to be working, return to love, always. Trust that the sign is something more than just a coincidence. It is love in its purest form. Notice coincidences in your life so that you can meet these people, who are so important to your life.

"With these signs complete, you have covered every detail you need and it is all perfect. When the day approaches for you to be born into human life, everyone gathers together. Hold one another and share in the love and light of the group. Your essence at this moment is one. You are one in purpose and one in intention. Everyone gives their energy and love to you. Everyone wishes more than anything for this life to be a great success for

you. Promise to do your best and to find your way home.

"A great pillar of light opens up to carry you to your destination, your life that awaits you here on Earth. As you step through, you look back on all of your loved ones, and hear their call...

"'REMEMBER... REMEMBER ... REMEMBER LOVE... REMEMBER CHOOSING... LOVE IS THE KEY... REMEMBER WHO YOU ARE... LOVE IS THE ONLY ANSWER... REMEMBER US... REMEMBER LOVE... REMEMBER... REMEMBER ...'

"Now you are here. Now you remember! For possibly the first time in your life, you remember. It matters not what you have done until this point in your life. Everything in your life is perfect. Everything in your life is a lesson to get you to this point in your life. It is all perfect. Now you know. Now you have the awareness. Now you have the knowledge of the signs and of your search. REMEMBER!

"You now trust in yourself. You now know the truth. You now have the keys. Whenever you need an answer in your life, all you have to do is remember to love and to trust. REMEMBER!

"See again the pillar of white light and love that now surrounds you. See the connection again from the universal source of love, flowing down through you and to the center of the Earth. Now see an enormous surge of that light come back up through the center of the pillar and back through the Earth and through the center of the pillar that surrounds you. When it reaches above your head, see it flower. Picture it forming an umbrella of white light above your head. See the umbrella of white light covering you and all those around you. See the edge of the umbrella sprinkling droplets of this white light, covering the entire area around you. Expand it outward, and see the umbrella of this white light covering the city, then the country, and eventually the entire planet around you. Feel this connection to your entire environment. See you as the conduit for love being spread around the entire globe. It only takes trust and wishing it to be so to create this. See these droplets of love and light, sending out a call to all of those in your soul group. See them know you, that this love has come from you, and that you are ready to remember them. You are ready to once again return to the path that you had chosen. Know that this is true! Know that this is already happening.

"Start to bring your consciousness back into your body. Take several deep relaxing breaths. As you breathe in, see even more of the love from this source filling every cell of your body. Feel the warmth and connection to all those around you. Feel at one with everyone in the room. Realize, just now, that anyone in your life is probably a part of your personal group. Now that you know to remember love, you will recognize them. If they are not part of your group, they are a part of another one. They are searching for their path and their destiny the best way they know how. Know that we are all here to learn from, and love one another.

"Take several more slow breaths. Feel yourself in a new state of awareness. Feel your body as every cell starts to flourish from this new state of awareness. Feel alive and awake in this new knowledge of your search. Feel enlivened with the knowledge that following your path is simply remembering love. As you come present, just now, you may open your eyes with this new knowledge of light and love.

"Look out with your awakened eyes and be aware of everyone in the room. REMEMBER LOVE! REMEMBER!"

As the facilitator finishes the meditation, a song begins to play about love. Melanie is crying softly. Her partner, Deanna is asleep. 'How can she sleep through this?' But interestingly, Melanie begins to see Deanna a little differently. 'She looks almost angelic sleeping like a child who has played so hard that no amount of noise disturbs her sleep. I wonder if she has played so hard in this life that she needs to sleep through love. It is so sad.' And with that thought, Melanie feels guilty for judging Deanna so harshly, especially if she has had such a hard life, and Melanie now sheds another few tears, this time for Deanna.

Melanie's mind has shifted to an expanded focus, a focus of love. In silence, in reflection, in expanded consciousness, Melanie's heart is opening a little space for understanding someone she never thought she could like. All the while, Deanna remains in a deep sleep, almost like a coma. But even in sleep, her mind is still hearing, and through hearing she may be changing.

Remember love?

Remembering love implies that you once knew about love but forgot. The next question might be, "When did I forget?"

When you imagine for a moment that you are standing in heaven before you are born, do you feel it? I am not saying that I know that you or I ever stood in a place called heaven before we were born, because of course, if we did stand in heaven, we have probably forgotten. However, I have spoken to people who say that they remember before they were born. You can even read their stories in books that have been written about near-death experiences, or heard about people who have been hypnotized. I hear people talk of past lives, and I have experienced a past life regression personally.

Does the mind create these stories? Who can really know at this point? I have noticed that in these past life stories, what a person encounters will usually reflect a significant issue that they are now experiencing in their life. For our purposes, this idea of a heavenly fantasy in meditation is designed primarily to expand your consciousness to encompass more of the world around you. This world that you miss is one you could sense, but have not been noticing. The world around you goes way beyond your ordinary sensory input.

Expand your mind and imagine standing in heaven before you were born. Then imagine that you are planning your upcoming life on Earth, including all the people you will meet here, like your parents, your friends, your children, your close relationships, your enemies, and all those you never notice. Imagine that you know about your life path and about your goal for deciding to have a life here. Really stretch your imagination, keeping in mind everything that has happened to you so far in this life. Then, imagine that you remember love as the reason for life.

If love is the reason for life, how much love have you forgotten, and how could you get back on track? What in this life keeps you from remembering love as a goal for life? What if your whole goal in life is to remember love?

The problem with remembering love is that you can get so distracted with your fear of love (adrenaline-charged survival responses) that love could become a very hazy goal, often just out of reach. It is as if you are only half-awake and half-dreaming, and you want to dream more instead of being awake. What would happen if you were to wake up and remember that you are dreaming about all the distractions of life, and then remember love is the focus? What if love is the only permanent condition? Then, your life would be one of awe and wonder. Then, your life would be one of compassion for the suffering of others. It could well be that distractions are creating suffering. Maybe within the loving focus, suffering would end.

As you wake up and see others still dreaming the distractions, you might experience pain both in empathy for others, and because you have the same pain in your life. Remembering love will not erase all pain. Compassion is holding the multidimensional focus of the dream and awakening together while you remember love.

At first when your heart opens, it often feels uncomfortable, as if it would break. It is very similar to the first time you exercise after you have not used a muscle. At first, it aches and tells you that you cannot use it. Then, after you continue to slowly use the muscle, the pain leaves and you have a new level of competency. Your heart will become accustomed to compassion, and you will wonder how you ever chose to be more concerned with distractions than love. And you will wonder how you ever possessed so many negative mental attitudes of judgment about people around you when people are obviously suffering from the distractions of forgetfulness, which you no longer have.

We talked in an earlier chapter about how distractions are what most of us call life. But what if you can imagine that love is really what this life is all about, and all you have to do is wake up and remember love? Then, all the choices in life would be based on love instead of the ego or fear. Then, all the distractions would obviously be distractions from love.

Love is the path of your soul. Imagine that love is the reason that you are here, and change your focus in that direction. The more you can imagine that love is the reason you are here, the more you will be able to align your choices to this focus. These choices are the ones that resonate with your purpose in life. When your goals are aligned to your life purpose of love, then your life will become one of endless love. Does this remind you of the music playing in the background? Listen for the songs of love all around you.

Carefully notice if you feel any pain. Pain and love are often linked, just like feeling compassion and suffering are often linked. Watch your focus. If you leave pain behind for one moment and feel only love, what would happen? It would be like a smooth lake with the sunlight glistening across the surface. Remember the focus. The focus of love is smooth and inspiring, just like the surface of that lake, or like gazing at the stars on a clear dark night.

And speaking of stars, the participants are finally leaving for the evening. They are stopping on the way to their rooms after a very long day, because they have one more short assignment besides the evening journal homework. They are gazing at the magnificent Sedona stars. The radiance of starlight will finish the evening and aid in connecting them to the vastness of the universe.

Chapter Six Journal Questions

1. What is your focus most of the time?
2. What do you fear about love? (Hint: Check out your body for tension, your mind for thoughts of loss or for beliefs about others.)
3. What do you feel in your body, and think in your mind about love?
4. What is your goal in life, and what have you been doing about your goals?
5. Do you remember love?
6. What happens when you attempt to remember love?
7. What songs are playing for you when you think about love?

Chapter 7 Breathing Destiny

Cellular Theta Breathing & Destiny

"And so faith is closing your eyes and following the breath of your soul down to the bottom of life, where existence and nonexistence have merged into irrelevance. All that matters is the little part you play in the vast drama."
–Real Live Preacher

"Destiny is no matter of chance. It is a matter of choice. It is not a thing to be waited for, it is a thing to be achieved."
–William Jennings Bryan (1860 - 1925)

Friday

Deanna's yawning actually surprises her. Most of her young adult life, Deanna's nights were filled with drinking binges, or most recently since being in recovery, late night television, or if she is lucky, phone calls with friends. Of course, a relationship with a man would cure everything in her mind, and even though she is actually in a relationship, it doesn't count in her mind because they are not married. As she likes to repeat, "I wouldn't marry that one even if he asks."

'Well, at least he could keep me from being so lonely; that is if this one counted as a relationship, and the man I keep company with does keep me company, but not exactly what I need so it doesn't really qualify as company in my mind. If only…'

Do you see how Deanna is creating a reality about men and about aloneness, and about friends, one that is quite impossible to fill? She dismisses the people she has in her life as not being enough, and looks for someone who will be enough, which is impossible to find because enough doesn't exist for her.

'I have never slept this much in years. Meditation is a cure for my insomnia. If I never get anything else out of this experience but the ability to sleep, I will be happy. I wonder why Melanie seems so much nicer since last night. She actually smiles at me and tries to communicate nonverbally. I thought she would be torturing me the whole time. This retreat is full of surprises.'

Melanie's thoughts seem to be tuning into Deanna's thoughts. 'I feel bad for treating Deanna so badly. I hope she didn't notice.' Melanie's hair is soft brown with highlights, but it has never been washed without being styled to perfection in public since childhood, until today. Now, it drapes around her face, giving her the appearance of a five-year-old. 'Thank God we weren't talking or she would be totally offended by what I would have said. This silence saved my butt. Maybe I could learn to stay silent all the time when I feel irritated with people. It has never occurred to me that I could actually hold back my energy and feel better for it. This silence is something else! But poor Deanna is sleeping a lot and missing some good stuff.' Melanie is still judging Deanna's experience, but she is also learning the value of silence. However, much of what she thinks, she forgets to write in her journal immediately after it happens, because her mind often runs amok with thoughts of judgment, or other thoughts without her noticing the negativity.

Continually forgetting about the way the mind thinks is one way you never realize how you are creating your reality. This is how you can miss the fact that you are creating your destiny.

This is how you can ignore the fact that you are creating emotions that are feeding energy into the creation of your life.

Melanie is reformatting her judgments of Deanna, but her mind is still fantasizing about what Deanna is doing. Whenever you decide that you know what is going on in another person's mind, you are really talking about yourself. Your mind's explanation of another is what would be going on if your mind was running the other person. The mind feels compelled to categorize everything that it finds significant. Melanie has a very anxious mind that is easily triggered into nervous, defensive thinking and action. She often exudes this energy to others, and others are creating stories to explain her energy to their mind's satisfaction.

When a trigger occurs, the mind can be instantaneously spurred into reaction, and the body pumps chemicals to accompany the emotional decision. With some minds, the space between a trigger and a reaction can be so small that it feels impossible for you to change your response to a trigger. You can increase the space between your emotional reactions, including the thoughts you have, as well as decrease your chemical reactions, which in turn will decrease the amount of time that it will take you to shift into a normal state of mind. You will find more space between your trigger and your reactions, along with a shorter reaction when you relax your exaggerated survival defenses.

Deanna and Melanie have been in silence while profoundly relaxing. Relaxation, meditations including movements like yoga or tai chi and breathing exercises are all ways in which you can take back your personal power. Relaxing your survival responses can restore your sense of well-being, giving needed oxygen to the brain during a crisis as it helps to heal your body. As soon as you relax your normal narrow way of thinking, you create a space for a new thought, a new creative way of viewing your world.

"Ouch!" Right now, Deanna is suffering with the morning stretching yogic exercises, being led by a woman who doesn't look like your normal yoga instructor. This voluptuous facilitator is contorting her body into stretches for the others to follow.

'How can she do these exercises and look happy? This hurts! How is this supposed to be relaxing? I need some coffee.' Deanna's question is a good one. Her mind is actually exaggerating her pain while telling her that she cannot do this activity. Not only is she deciding that she cannot do the exercise, she is also in disbelief that the instructor is enjoying herself. With this type of exercise, the pain increases as you fight the movement. Her mind is rebelling, tightening her muscles, and causing additional pain.

"Breathe in through your nose, slowly and stretch while holding your breath. Now, exhale and release." The instructor takes the group through a system of mild stretches, tapping, and their first instructions about breathing. This activity can help to release toxins, relax tension, and improve energy flow before starting a day of Cellular Theta Breathing, guided meditations, and other activities.

This day will be one of transformation. To begin with, this type of exercise will help the physical body's stamina while beginning the expansion of the mind for the day. Even though Deanna and others may feel a little pain when stretching beyond their normal range of motion, the pain rarely causes soreness the next day. The effects are subtle and will be missed by many of the participants. Like most exercise, you often only notice the results after you practice for a week or more. Fortunately, you will be able to instantly notice how great you feel from tapping and breathing, but the mind may be so obsessed with discomfort that you never notice anything but your complaining mind.

The goal, which is explained in the beginning of the exercise activity, is to focus on your body and your energy. The goal is not to perform the exercise perfectly. The most important thing in this exercise is to focus on the release of energy at the end of your exhale. Deanna, like many, focuses on pain and on judging herself and others. As usual, she also dwells on escape of the pain, much of which she is creating with her thoughts. If she follows instructions and if she can remember to notice her thoughts rather than participating with them, she will be writing about her mind talk after the exercises, and noticing the themes of how much she cannot tolerate discomfort. This sneaky mental creation also makes a plausible excuse for her almost constant need to escape. The wish for escape in this case would be her desire for coffee, a mind-stimulating painkilling drug.

Melanie has a different set of thoughts racing through her mind, although they are also about judgment. 'I can do this one and most of the other participants cannot! Well, if they went to the gym every day like I do, they would lose some of that weight and be able to perform too. How can people stand being out of shape like that? Wow, this one hurts! The instructor must not know how to lead this exercise correctly. She certainly could use the gym. I bet her body has never seen the inside of one. Why don't they get a really physically fit instructor to lead these exercises, one who takes better care of herself? She is a bad role model for exercise. I better do this exercise minimally in case she is showing us the wrong way so I don't hurt my back.'

Melanie is once again obsessing with judging others and feeling superior, and once again, she hasn't noticed that her mind is creating a reality of separation. She doesn't think to write this mind talk because this type of thought is like the water in a fish tank to the fish. It is ever-present and she swims here all the time.

At the retreat, we use a combination of types of energy exercises. These exercises help you become of aware of the flow of energy in and around your body, increasing your positive flow of energy while you participate in ever-expanding states of consciousness.

The participants will experience many mind-altering activities, one of the most profound of which is Cellular Theta Breathing. But before we talk more about Cellular Theta Breathing, let's first take a look at a couple of other examples of breathing techniques, all of which are transformational.

Breathing

Taking a deep breath is one of the fastest ways to reduce fear. Are you ready to practice some techniques for reducing the release of your adrenaline, and taking charge of your survival defenses? Take a long deep breath. Every time you get stressed, angry, or in other words, in fear, take a slow deep breath. Then, exhale for a long time. If your thoughts are running on without your conscious awareness, then you may also be unconsciously avoiding situations of personal growth to avoid feeling out of control. You could also be so controlled by fear that you feel you have no choice other than avoidance. Even worse, you may be carrying a load of fear, all the while staying unconscious of your stress. Your fearful, shallow breathing in that case would feel to you as if you are 'normal.' Fear of emotional pain, physical pain, or just plain discomfort could be undermining your ability to find meaning in your life. At the very least, you might like to accomplish some goal in life that you presently fear, like flying to an exotic vacation destination. Learning breathing techniques can help you relax and enjoy activities you previously feared. Relaxation can remove anxiety, panic, and discomfort when trying new activities. Ultimately, you can achieve a sense of empowerment by being able to manage your own survival chemicals effortlessly.

Breathing deeply begins the relaxation of your automatic survival mechanism. Of course, if you are in real danger, and by real I mean real physical danger or ongoing mental and emotional stress, you can use all the adrenaline charged chemical cocktails to defend yourself.

You are pumping some of these chemicals whenever you feel stress throughout the day. Shallow breathing accompanies ongoing daily stress, because one of the responses of the body is to tighten the chest and abdominal wall. With enough of this stress, you can actually feel like you are almost suffocating. Two or three deep breaths decrease these feelings, and can lower your blood pressure. Breathe and begin to relax. Learning to relax helps you to feel more powerful than you could ever imagine, and gives you the ability to aim your life in unknown directions of joy.

Breath is life. You can live without water for hours, food for days, shelter for who knows how long, but breathing is an instantaneous necessity! Our denial about our quality of breathing is immense. Because you breathe automatically, unless you are choking, have asthma, or a cold, you are most likely taking breathing for granted. The body breathes for you, without thought. How often do you stop and notice your breath? Your breathing pattern is linked to your environment, to the planet itself, to the past, to the present, and to the creation of your future. A breath pattern emerges to accompany every event of your life. Your body and mind remember the breath pattern you had during significant events in your life. The memory of an event recalls the same body memories that accompanied the original occurrence.

When you become aware that you are gasping, with a deep inhale as if you are being punched in the stomach, in anticipation of the future, you can become terrified about your inability to get yourself under control. Think about a time when you were shocked. You inhaled, and then what? The long sigh usually occurs when you are finally relieved of the shock. Teaching your body a new pattern; the pattern of inhaling and exhaling slowly in a long deep relaxing breath will give you a new response every time you feel stressed, angry, or terrified. Add that to the breathing that is relaxing the muscles of your body, and you have fully directed your mind to remember a technique for handling discomfort in the future. Keep repeating this deep breathing, relaxation technique every time you feel fear or anger, which is just another manifestation of fear, and within a couple of months, you will have an automatic reaction known as the relaxation response. It is like installing a new program in the computer that automatically fixes a glitch that bothers you on your computer. Once installed, you will instantly begin to relax whenever you experience adrenaline reactions. With a little extra oxygen, your mind will function at its full potential when you most need your brain.

Stop and think about air for minute. You are breathing a conglomeration of gases, primarily nitrogen, along with every other air-breathing creature. The plants are taking in the waste that you exhale and then producing more air for the planet. We are all breathing each other's air! You are actually breathing the cellular content that is exhaled from others. As you exhale, you are exhaling part of your body! As you inhale, you inhale material from others! We all notice smells, but how often have you thought exactly how interrelated you are through the air that is being shared?

Like most people, you are probably ignoring the importance of air; that is unless you are listening to the ecologists talk about the demise of the rainforest. Take a break and imagine that the planet is healed, that the rainforest is creating lots of life-giving oxygen, and that we are getting rid of our pollution.

A smoker is beyond ignoring air quality. Since air is giving you life, then smoke-filled, polluted air is depriving you of your life force. Your life force is compromised. Denial is the only way that one can smoke and forget about the damage.

Think about the job of plants on this planet. They are our air producers. We are interdependent in a world that seems to be disconnected. Plants and breathing are only one of the infinite connections that go unnoticed as we go about our daily lives. As you acknowledge more and more connections, you begin to experience the state of oneness; or the exact opposite of the state of loneliness. Relief floods through the body, a sigh escapes your lungs, and every muscle starts releasing until you resemble a soft cloth doll. Remember to consistently practice and aim for this state of being. Tell yourself that you are swimming in a sea of connected energy, connected with everything in creation, then breathe deeply, sigh, and release tension in every muscle in your body. You are never alone.

Consciously changing your breathing pattern will alter the way you think and feel. If you study different cultures and methods for enlightenment, you will find various ways of manipulating the breath pattern in order to transform your consciousness. Around the world, breathing techniques are practiced as a means of finding enlightenment. Even if you are not actively seeking a state of enlightenment, you could benefit physically, mentally, and emotionally by practicing breathing techniques.

Now let's explore a couple of formal breathing meditation and healing techniques. These techniques have several potential benefits; one of the most important is the improvement of your health. If you are one of many chronic sufferers of anxiety, then you can use the simplest of breathing techniques to relieve your symptoms. If you desire to uncover blocked emotions and find significant life-altering memories, then you can practice rebirthing breathing. If you desire expansion of consciousness, states of bliss and enlightenment, practice breathing meditations such as Cellular Theta Breathing.

(NOTE: You can practice the following breathing techniques alone, with the exception of rebirthing. Rebirthing can create deep emotional activation and requires a facilitator. Optimally, a trained professional therapist is best when practicing rebirthing for your safety.)

Instant Help for Stress

Take a deep breath through your nose and very slowly exhale through your mouth, blowing out for longer than you inhale, emptying your lungs completely. Take another breath just like that one, and if you feel really stressed, one more. This simple breathing pattern can lower your blood pressure when it is soaring due to stress. This is a good practice anytime you find yourself in an anxious or painful state of mind. The task is to remember to take a long deep breath when you need it! Use it for stress, anxiety, anger, and sadness. Strong emotions take your breath away. Practice taking your breath back! Essentially, taking the slowest inhales and slowest exhales; breathing slower and slower will create relaxation and reduce the flow of anxiety producing chemicals. Watch and think breathing.

Watching the Pause – Mindful Breathing

This breath technique is quite simple and works well for many situations, especially for relieving mental obsessions. All you need for this activity is a quiet, comfortable place. Make sure that all your bodily needs are taken care of. Relax in a comfortable position. Take normal breaths. The first lie that your mind could tell you is that you cannot breathe normally if you pay attention to your breathing. This statement is a lie. Tell the mind thank you, but that you are breathing normally now.

(NOTE: If paying attention to your breath causes you to panic, don't worry. You can learn to breathe slowly through another form of meditation we will practice later in the book.)

Next, pay attention to your inhale and exhale of the normal breath pattern, as well as the small pauses in the pattern, which you could call no-breath. Watch the breath pattern for a minute or so, identifying the pauses, the places when you are neither inhaling nor exhaling. Begin shifting your consciousness to observe only the pauses in your normal breath pattern. Continue watching the pauses. When your mind chatter begins, and you get distracted, just tell the mind, "Not right now, I am watching the pauses in my breath." Observe your mind chatter as if it is passing you by like a cloud floating by, without getting distracted from your task of watching the pause in your breath. Thoughts float by. Continue placing your consciousness within the pause in your breath. If after a few minutes you find that you are totally distracted by your thoughts, just stop your thought at that moment, and begin to observe the pauses once again. Make a little mental note about the type of thoughts that are distracting you, along with how these thoughts affect your tension and breathing.

If you worry because you keep losing focus, tell yourself that being distracted by thoughts is your normal way of functioning. It is normal for your mind to run amok. Watching your breath is not your normal behavior. With any breathing exercise, you are swimming against the current of your own lack of awareness. Usually, the mind does not wish to alter its normal behavior without constant prodding. The mind is quite opinionated, and accustomed to its position of unrestrained thinking. Keep refocusing the mind on the pause in your breath.

Congratulations, you are meditating! Buddha is said to have

found enlightenment through becoming mindful of his inhale and exhale. (Ananda Sutta) You can find this same enlightenment by becoming completely aware of your breath pattern: inhale and exhale. When you are mindful, you are completely absorbed into the moment of the breath pattern and present in all your daily activities. Simply being totally involved in walking, eating, and every activity, you will find the peace that you already possess.

Most likely you will not find enlightenment the first time you do it. Even if you never reach a state of enlightenment, you could find a little peace of mind. Observe the mind chatter and you will observe how your thoughts trigger emotions. Observe the breathing pattern and you will see the link between your thoughts, emotions, and the alteration of your breathing. As you are breathing and observing the mind, you are now creating enough distance so that you can notice the themes of your mind's ongoing litany about your world, which is creating your reality, your destiny.

For example, my mind likes to talk to me about my so-called negative, anxious, and depressing problems. When I first tried this meditation, I was very impatient. I was also very unhappy. My mind was thinking about negative, depressing, anxiety-producing thoughts. I would hear things like, 'That guy you're dating doesn't really like you.' Or, 'You will never have enough money.' Pretty depressing stuff would be floating through my mind as I looked for pauses in the breathing. As I would think these depressing thoughts, my emotions would intensify and my breathing would become shallow. My body would feel tense and painful. Then, I would begin to feel more anxious, sometimes even with feelings of panic. As I returned to observing a normal breathing pattern, my anxiety would fade away. I actually already knew that my mind talked to me with depressing, anxious thoughts because I had learned some mind stopping techniques. In other words, as a therapist, I knew how to divert my mind to stop that talk and focus on something else. But I still had the beliefs and themes in my mind, waiting for my stillness to create a space for the chatter to begin. This ongoing mental torment is why people don't like to be alone, in silence.

One day, as I was observing this mental garbage while meditating on the pauses, I had a spontaneous spark of enlightenment. In the midst of my depressing mind talk, my observer self looked around at the present situation. I was sitting in my office. It was a very nice office, pleasant paintings, furniture, colors, etc. It smelled great and the temperature was perfect, even though outside it was about 112 degrees. In the present moment, I really had no problems except the ones created by my mind chatter. Next, I realized one of the best insights of my life. "I have no problems at this moment as long as I have my next breath."

By silencing my negative thoughts and focusing on my breath, I began to laugh! Laughter is stress reduction at its best! This is one of those times that stretches into a long moment, and is embedded into a memory that fills me with joy to this day, many years later. It will stay with me forever as a defining moment of my life.

But do not think that I meditated for years on end to get this insight. I had tried this breath meditation a couple of times in a few spare minutes at work! Insights can arrive quickly when you are aware and mindful of the present. When you are mindful, your energy can shift to positive or neutral. Then your life, and consequently your future will reflect that shift.

Observing life beyond the mind chatter is in itself a form of stress reduction. Adding the component of the breath to observation increases the effectiveness of the meditation. Remember that breath is your life. Once you get to the level of life and death, many of your needs, thoughts, problems, and wants cease. All you have left is peace. Become totally present and peace arrives.

Rebirthing

As I was already being completely impressed with the blood pressure lowering breath, and looking for pauses in the breath, I was offered the opportunity to learn another type of breathing known as rebirthing. I wasn't really given an option in the matter, and I wasn't at all that happy about learning this breath technique. The supervisor I had at the time made this event a requirement for her program. I either had to take it or argue my way out of it. As a therapist in training, you learn very early on that arguing is called resistance. How can one be a therapist, a person who will ask others to go past resistance and dive into the depths of the unconscious muck if you yourself are unwilling to go within? In other words, argument is out of the question.

You would think that since I had a negative mind, lots of defenses, and high anxiety, I would be jumping at a chance to learn a new breath process. But changing the breath pattern can be frightening. I was afraid. Of course, anyone who knows me knows that I am generally afraid a lot! In fact, I keep telling my friends that everything I do is a near-death experience to me, but I don't think they get it. Do you? Altering the breath for expansion of consciousness and for catharsis - releasing emotions - brings up some serious defense mechanisms, and in fact, it brings up suppression of breathing, which sounds a whole lot like suffocation to my mind.

Rebirthing is an intense breathing experience. It can reduce stress, release physical, mental, and emotional memories, increase oxygenation of the body, and is extremely activating, and by activation I am talking about emotional activation.

My advice is that if you want to do rebirthing, have a good

licensed psychotherapist present. Rebirthing can trigger intense psychological responses. If you have entrenched fear, rebirthing may help remove it. However, Cellular Theta Breathing, which I will be discussing next, will remove fear in a less intense fashion over a longer period of time.

Leonard Orr (Orr, 1977) is the author of rebirthing, and you can check out several books on the subject for a more in-depth study. It is named rebirthing because it can trigger a memory of your birth, and you could relive your birth, according to the authors. I have witnessed and had this experience of birth while participating in a breath session. But the most advantageous breath sessions I have had didn't involve my birth into this world. These sessions were more like giving birth to my true self.

If requested, I still facilitate a rebirthing session, although now I prefer the Cellular Theta Breathing that we practice at Destiny, and in weekly groups, because I feel that it is a gentler process. In the business of psychology, rebirthing is like a Gestalt type of technique, which basically means that the person could encounter a piece of unfinished psychological information, and could then process it to its completion. The reason I am giving the warning about having a therapist in the room is that some but not all rebirthers, don't know how to process a memory of a severe nature. A properly trained rebirther can process with a participant, but an improperly trained one can create problems. I have seen several clients after they experienced an incomplete rebirthing experience. I have had one myself. When they came to therapy, they were convinced that they were going crazy. Being stuck in an emotional experience can be scary, and can feel like insanity. Feeling like you are losing your mind doesn't mean that you are. That feeling is often a ploy of the mind, a defense to keep you away from unpleasant memories. However, once stuck in this ploy, you may be incapacitated for a while.

Now, if it sounds like I don't like rebirthing, you are right. Who likes to uncover the garbage they are hiding in the depths of defense? I think it is a powerful tool for releasing fear. I don't like the dentist either, but the alternative is unacceptable! Avoidance of fear means that fear continues to run your life. Rebirthing is a way to walk through the source of your fearfulness. I know from my own experience that rebirthing significantly and permanently decreased my fear.

Before rebirthing, I could never sleep alone in the dark. After several rebirthing sessions, at the age of thirty-six, I could finally sleep in the dark. If you have any irrational fears such as this fear of the dark, rebirthing can help you release it.

Releasing old fears is a noble goal. When you refuse to release old fears, they tend to become more and more debilitating as you age. You are stuck in a rut, the walking dead. Continual personal growth is the road out of the rut. Release old fears. Love and accept yourself, and you will be living the full life. You will be moving forward on the road of life, and you will be awake. You will be living in the light. If you try to stand still to keep your life the same, you will fall backwards.

How do you do rebirthing anyway? It is a breath technique in which you take deep connected breaths for about twenty minutes or more. As you continue breathing in and out, with your chest rising and falling, you will find that your favorite fearful defenses begin to emerge inside of you. In this breath pattern, you do not allow a pause between your inhale and exhale. You can have intense physical pain and tension as your emotions struggle for expression. You may encounter emotional blocks that you have lived with for many years, blocks to feelings, blocks of physical memories of past events, and even full-blown recollections of past occurrences during the session. A note about repressed memories; they aren't exactly to be taken literally in every case. I suggest you look at them symbolically, much like you would interpret a dream.

In the end, you can feel very relieved. It usually takes about three hours to complete the process. I allow a minimum of one and one half-hours for a session itself, and it could take three days or more to fully incorporate the event into your life. When transforming an old belief into a new awareness, the mind takes a couple of days to sort of reformat the connections. Use rebirthing for releasing fear. However, after you have freed yourself from repression of fear and emotion, you can find enlightenment and experiences of bliss with rebirthing.

Rebirthing is an intense method that demonstrates how profoundly you can alter your consciousness just by altering your breath pattern. Remember that you have a breath pattern memorized for every event in your life. When you have been stressed in your life, you have locked that breath pattern into your memory. Unlocking your breath patterns, learning that you can obtain oxygen when you are emotionally triggered, you are once again free.

Now, let's go back to the seminar and check in on our favorite participants for a minute.

'What now?' Melanie is feeling nervous for some reason. She doesn't know what is coming up next, but feels some kind of vague discomfort about it. Deanna, on the other hand, is already getting sleepy. Both of them are fluffing their sleeping bags, and preparing to recline in comfort as they wait for the next activity. There is a little buzz in the air, and the facilitators are all standing around the room as if they are positioning themselves for something important. The way the facilitators have themselves positioned in the room, they almost look like the secret service surrounding the perimeter for the person at the front of the room. Candles are lit, as they were the night before, and a floating aroma of lavender and something exotic wafts through the air. The air is heavy. Standing at the front of the room, a soft-spoken blond facilitator begins an explanation of the upcoming breath meditation.

'Janna is lying down like she knows it all. Well, I guess she has already done this retreat, and like seeing a comedy for the second time, she knows all the jokes before they happen. She looks really relaxed. I just don't see how she can look so happy the whole time. Doesn't she still get bugged by these people, or by her mind, or anything?' Melanie is still judging, while Deanna is getting more and more sleepy.

Are you beginning to see that the patterns of mental defenses just keep happening over and over, as if humans are all stuck in a vicious cycle of sameness? The mind keeps dragging out its tricks over and over. Why would it come up with something new when the same old easy defensiveness and addictions keep working again and again? Remember that your search for ecstasy may be your attachment to dysfunction rather than bliss.

The facilitator begins her explanation about Cellular Theta Breathing. This is the breath meditation used throughout the retreat, but before the first breath session, the new participants need some instructions.

Cellular Theta Breathing

THE BREATH EXPLANATION

"Cellular Theta Breathing is a profound breathing technique designed to facilitate an inner journey. The technique itself is not new. Breathing exercises are ancient, and can be found in many disciplines including yoga, tai chi, qigong, and martial arts of all types.

"The breath is also known as prana, which means life force. Think about the quality and quantity of your breathing right now. Most of us breathe in a shallow and unconscious way. The more emotionally triggered you become, the more your breath can be disrupted. You may breathe rapidly and hyperventilate, or you may hold your breath until you feel suffocated. When you are triggered, you can tell yourself to breathe when you are having an intense emotion. If you are observant, you can tell that someone is triggered by watching his or her breathing.

"If the breath is life force, and obviously you have no life if you have no breath, then altering the breath alters your experience of life. In Cellular Theta Breathing, you will be taking in additional air, breathing very deeply for about five minutes until you ideally enter a theta state of consciousness. Then you remain in and out of the theta state for about fifty minutes. The theta state is the state of consciousness in which dreaming occurs. Right now, if you are wide awake and thinking, you are in the beta state. If you are profoundly relaxed as in meditation, you enter the alpha state. In deep dreamless sleep, you enter delta, the state closest to death. These states of consciousness refer to brainwave pulses, like a heartbeat, and can be measured in hertz, which is the speed of the pulses. The beta state is the most rapid, and the delta is the slowest. There are actually some higher states, and possibly some lower ones, but we are simplifying our discussion to the common brainwave states that you experience.

"As you move from alpha to theta, you are pulsing at a rate that matches the frequency rate of the Earth, or more accurately, the cavity between the Earth and its magnetic field known as the Schumann resonance region. When you are aligned with that rate, that frequency, you often feel much more connected to the Earth. This matching experience appears to have a profoundly healing affect on humans and their relationship with the world. Whenever you achieve a point of empathy, you are on track for creating a personal destiny of peace. You will receive the same energy that you are emanating. Theta is an energy frequency that will change your life when you become conscious of it, that is when you become capable of decreasing your brainwaves when you wish. You have been experiencing theta your whole life. Now is your opportunity to become aware of it, and all the benefits of that awareness.

"The benefits of pulsing at the same rate as the Earth are numerous. One such benefit is that you will no longer be as influenced by the mass of human energy functioning in beta. In other words, a crowded negative social setting will have no effect on your mood when you are tuned in to the relaxed brainwave that matches the Earth. You will have peace in the face of discord. Your energy field may feel out of sync with the world's reality, as you become in sync with the underlying energy of reality. Your peaceful energy can influence those around you to relax as well. Brainwaves are contagious, and influence the energy around you.

"Dolphins and babies are living in a theta state. If you ever get a chance to be around dolphins, try the Cellular Theta breath in their presence. Once you enter theta, the dolphins may acknowledge you. At that point, you are experiencing a type of interspecies communication through a brainwave state. I am not alone in having the experience of wild dolphins seeking my company while in theta. A mature dolphin and an immature dolphin appearing to be a mother and child swam over to a group of us practicing theta one day. Both of them were part of a pack of dolphins hunting nearby. These two rolled over and showed us their bellies. Then, as the adult started back to hunt, the young one appeared to have a little tantrum about leaving, slapping a tail fin hard against the water. I felt like they were observing our theta experiment, like we observe apes in a zoo, and the child was not finished looking.

"Remember also, the dream state is a state of consciousness in which the mind heals itself. Within theta, you could experience profound mental healing, but that is not all. You may encounter lucid dreaming and an expanded state of consciousness, in which words suddenly fail to describe the experience (Hardgrave, 2003). The closest approximation of a description for me would be to use the word mystical, a direct experience of God, or the Oneness of the universe.

"Watch me and follow along as I demonstrate the breath. First, blow out all of your air. Next, visualize taking in a long inhale from the base of your spine, all the way up to about twelve inches above your head. To accomplish such a long inhale, take almost a second inhale at the throat while tilting the head back a little to open up the airway. In adults, tilting the neck back opens the airway. In young children, tilting the neck back can restrict the airway. Breathe with your mouth open. Go ahead and make some breathing noises. Relax your jaw. Close your eyes. No one but facilitators will see you once we begin. The second part of the breath inhalation pattern sounds like you are catching your breath, as you take a second inhale when you tilt your head back. When you exhale, visualize sighing through your heart. (The facilitator is continually demonstrating.)

"Keep practicing the breath. Blow your air out. Let's try about three of those deep breaths. The objective is to imagine drawing in lots of oxygen, and imagining that you are drawing it up from the base of your spine all the way up through your spinal column, out of the top of your head, until you feel about twelve inches above your head. Practice this technique with an open mind, placing all your thoughts on your breathing. After a couple of these deep breaths, you may be feeling a little dizzy. Relax. This sensation passes with practice. Most people are unaccustomed to deep breathing. When you are doing this breath session for the first time, take a few of the deep breaths at various times throughout the music. Breathe deeply for as long as possible in the beginning, up to about five minutes maximum, give or take a couple of minutes. Take some more deep breaths here and there as you choose, when you feel you want to experiment with it. Entering theta, you would be dreaming and the breath then becomes irrelevant to you.

"If you find yourself tense or thinking, let your thoughts drift by like floating clouds, and focus on the music. The brainwave state is contagious. Since the facilitators and others in the room will be in a lower brainwave frequency, that will influence you as well. Relax. There is no right or wrong experience.

"You can sit up or lie down.

"All the facilitators will be matching your breath pattern with you. We match this breath as a form of empathy, and find ourselves picking up your energy as we do. The facilitators are energy healers, meaning that we are able to sense your energy and help you to move it. We will be circulating around the room, checking on you and working with your energy. We will be fluffing the energy around your body. If you have any discomfort or questions, please ask us. We are here to assist you. We may slightly touch you, but most likely we will work above you, and you will sense us by your side.

"Sometimes, you may experience discomfort or pain. We consider that this may be an energy block somewhere in your body where you may carry your tension. If this happens, take another deep breath and imagine that you are sending a white light and air to that spot. Then, completely relax. This breath has been known to completely relieve pain. Sometimes because of sadness or pent up emotions, you may cry or as the facilitators lovingly say, 'your eyes may leak.' Crying does not happen every time. Breath sessions are different and each one is your unique experience."

As she ends her explanation, the facilitators are walking around the room watching the participants practice the breath.

They stop to help people master the technique.

"Lie down and make yourself comfortable. If you need to go to the bathroom, get a drink, or have a need, then go ahead and make sure that you are totally comfortable before we begin."

When everyone is finally settled in and comfortable, the music begins to play. In the background of this unusual instrumental, another facilitator begins what sounds almost like a prayer.

PRAYER

"Please imagine that you can surround yourself and everyone in the room with a violet, blue, green, yellow, orange, red, and golden white light. Imagine that the light brings you safety, peace, and enlightenment. Call forth that light to surround and protect everyone in the room, including you. When you breathe in, breathe in the light. When you breathe out, breathe out the tension. Sigh through your heart with each exhale. Look deeply inside and call forth your own higher self, your higher power, your own angel or personal guide. Call forth God as you know God to be. Ask for protection and guidance. Ask for assistance in healing whatever issues you wish to heal. Place forth any intentions you may have, and then release them with a breath to be aligned with your highest good in life.

May everything that comes forth for you come from the highest source for your highest good. May everything that you release be released back to the source to be transmuted. May you find your way home today as you breathe in the light and the air. May you hear the still small voice of enlightenment from within. May you find bliss in the breath today."

For a while, all you can hear is the music playing quite loud, with the deep exhaling and inhaling of the participants, until one by one they fall silent into their dream-like meditative trances.

In the corner of her mind, she sees a beckoning light in the darkness, a luminous light amidst infinite black. She is smitten with this little speck of light in the distance, and feels that she can move her consciousness toward that source of light through her intention to move. It is as if she was flying with her mind, free-floating without a body, able to move in any direction because she willed it. As she wills herself toward the light, she speeds off in that direction, but just as quickly, the light flees from her pursuit, rushing ahead of her just out of reach. 'Darn it.' She stops. The light stops. She moves toward it. The light moves away. Her curiosity seems to be pushing that light away. 'What is happening to me in this breath meditation,' she is thinking, a lucid dream obviously since she can think about the breath session and have this vision of the moving light object at the same time, because the light is still glistening in the distance as she thinks? 'It feels like I am hallucinating. Wow! This is really cool! Ok, I will just hold still and allow the light to reveal itself to me.'

Whoosh, an angel appears suddenly from the middle of the luminous ball of starlight that was so far away a millisecond ago. The light appears to be a tunnel entrance of some sort, like a wormhole transporter for angels, one of whom is now in front of her nose. 'Oh, my God!' Deanna is stunned by the enormous face of an angel flying forth into her face so close that she can sense a luminous breath blowing air into her face as the angel begins to speak. "Deanna, you will learn to facilitate this breath. You will become a counselor and a healer."

'Me?' And then Deanna thinks maybe they have subliminal messages in the music, but no, how can they have subliminal visions unless everyone is seeing and hearing the same directions? Then, she is stunned into silence and drifts into deep

delta states of sleep.

Next to Deanna, Janna is peacefully seeing colors and feeling a deep state of relaxation, drifting in and out of sleep-like states of nothingness.

Melanie is thinking and thinking and thinking.

"I don't get what my mind is supposed to be doing. I don't think I am doing this right. I should be more relaxed. If I were doing this breath the right way, I would not be thinking at all. I would be out of it, I think. What is wrong with me? I am so bad at all this meditation stuff. Maybe they should have explained it longer and in more detail. I wish I could have asked more questions, but with all this silence, I would feel stupid talking because maybe they would just think I want to talk and talk. I hate when everyone talks when they are supposed to be quiet Why can't people follow the rules? I remember I always hated that when I was a little girl. At school, when I was doing my work, other kids would be talking. How did they ever learn anything talking all the time like that? It is a wonder that people ever get anywhere in life if they cannot follow any rules. When I have children, I will teach them to follow rules so they won't be annoying to others. That is the problem with people today, no one follows rules and no one cares about what is right and wrong. Wait a minute. What is that? Who is that little boy over there? He looks like someone I should know. Is that a little boy I knew when I was little? Maybe all this thinking about following rules and school reminded me of someone I used to know when I was about... well how old is he anyway?'

"I'm five," he answers her.

Melanie is taken back that he spoke to her. "Well, thank you. Do I know you?"

"Not yet," he says.

"What do mean, not yet?"

Melanie is feeling confused now. How can a child be in her mind that she has never met but remind her of someone she has never met?

"I must be dreaming. Oh yes, they said you could dream while doing that Cellular Breath. Oh good, it must be working because I am talking to a child in a dream I am having, and I know that I am dreaming! Wow! This kid reminds me of my husband Jack a little bit. That's it. He reminds me of Jack. Maybe I am seeing him as a child. Is this him like some picture I saw when he was a child? Wait, he says I haven't met him yet. Does that mean I am going to meet him? Oh come on, this is just a dream, but still I could ask him about what he means, right? No harm in checking out this dream I am having. They say dreams always mean something.

"OK, am I going to meet you?" *she asks, a little tenuously because it sort of makes her feel self-conscious to talk to a dream five-year-old child in a dream. But she feels very comfortable around this little boy. After all, he looks a lot like Jack...*

"Oh yes, you are my mother," *he says.*

Melanie feels her heart open and a joy pour forth like she never remembers feeling in her whole life. 'Never, never in my life have I felt this much happiness about hearing a few words, and here I am being thrilled by a dream child. If only this were true.'

"Oh I am true all right," *he says, reading her thoughts.* "I am your little boy. You are my mother and I am going to see you very soon." *He seems very convincing and certain of himself.*

'He has my personality I see, even if he looks like my husband! Oh, Jack is going to love our son! Good grief, listen to me getting all excited over a dream son... like he is real. Well, it sure feels real. This is some wishful dreaming I am having! Wow, this is how I would feel about a baby? I wonder what I *should name him'.*

"My name is Matthew," *he states in her mind.*

'*I guess in dreams people communicate telepathically. That is convenient. Matthew is the name I wanted for my first son and I guess this is my dream.*'

"Matthew, I love you." *Her statement of love shocks her.*

Melanie feels so much love that it is as if she cannot stand it anymore and has to tell him how much she loves him. She has never felt these kinds of loving feelings toward anyone before, and is surprised about the intensity of her feelings for a dream son. With those words, she wraps her arms around her child, holds him tenderly, and tears begin to roll silently down her checks. She can feel someone real standing outside her dream handing her a tissue, and wiping her tears, but she stays in her dream with her son because she is not ready to leave him just yet, not when she has just found him.

Cellular Theta Breathing is my favorite form of breathing meditation. However, I have had my resistance to it. As I said before, breathing in a way that is different from your normal way of breathing can be annoying, to say the least. The mind often fights the change.

What does Cellular Theta Breathing mean? Cellular refers to the cellular impact of the breath. Memories are not held only in the brain. All cells have memory. This breath technique theoretically can access the memory of the cells and activate memory and emotion in a way similar to rebirthing. However, this technique varies because it is also concerned with the attainment of a theta state of consciousness, dreaming additional dreams for the day.

Theta is that state of consciousness in which you are dreaming, and can be a very comforting state like that sweet place you attain right before you get up in the morning, when you know you are dreaming and you know you are sleeping. As the facilitator explained to the participants, state of consciousness actually refers to the number of pulses in the brainwave. Have you ever noticed that you have many states of consciousness? In deep sleep, the closest state to death known as delta, you are unaware, unconscious, and only know it by the absence of knowing. Above that state of consciousness is theta, the brainwave of dreaming, which is the goal of the breathing session. This breath technique is designed to propel you into the theta state. Within the theta state, when you experience lucid dreaming or visions, most of us remember some if not all of this state of mind. During Cellular Theta Breath, the visions will vary and are filled with some of the same types of symbols that you often see when dreaming at night. These visions can also be filled with symbols or beings that you may have never experienced in your dreams. You may see yourself in what appears to be a past life, reflecting activities or emotional motivations that are important to your current life. You can visit other realms that are indescribable. Dreams can be prophetic.

As you are lucidly dreaming, you are also aware that you can alter the course of your dream. However, control in theta often has the opposite effect than you may be trying to achieve, like when Deanna tried to catch her light by controlling it. Or you may be able to prolong your dream like when Melanie stayed to spend time with her child in her dream. Did you notice that when Melanie was dreaming, she was aware of the person handing her a tissue, but didn't leave her dream to wake up because she wasn't ready to leave yet? You can have awareness of the dream and awareness of the room around you, and other ordinary thoughts all at the same time. One cannot predict. One can only experience and observe.

Weekly, the staff of Destiny Retreats offers a Cellular Theta Breath class in my office. After the class, everyone shares their experiences, including details of some of the dreams. The main reason for sharing these experiences is to allow the participant time to fully awaken before returning home. Theta is not a good state of consciousness for operating machinery, especially moving vehicles. Most of us are aware that we need some time to become fully awake before driving. At Destiny, the participants don't discuss the session, but instead they use their journals so that they can stay with their silence after the breath session. They also practice the breath approximately five times over the long weekend, which gives them the cumulative affect of the breath and theta. They begin to stay in a slower brainwave frequency, relaxed and feeling more connected with nature around them as the retreat progresses.

In years of hearing theta dreams and visions, I have witnessed many miracles. A yoga instructor once said after attending one of our classes that Cellular Theta Breathing is the fastest breath technique for enlightenment that he had ever encountered. He began incorporating this breath into his regular yoga classes as a result. If you know anything about yoga, then you know that breathing is very important in the practice. Increasing the life force, prana is a goal of yogic practice.

Another miracle that I often witness is in the prophetic nature of the experiences. Sometimes, participants have reported talking to beings that tell of the future. Then, the event happens. I don't think that every time I hear something about the future that it will occur, because the mind is symbolic, difficult to interpret at times.

It is tempting to say that a person is creating the future event. Of course, this can be true! After all, as soon as you hear, see, and experience it in your dreams, you are in the creative state of making an event occur. I have at this time in my life decided that if an angel appears to me in a breath session, and says that I am going to Greece, then I am going to give some careful thought to participating in the creation of the trip, like updating my passport. I make it a practice to avoid any advice that is not based on love. If a fearful thought occurs within the breath or my daily life, I immediately begin relaxing. Remember, slow inhale, slow exhale, and relax to reduce fear and pain.

Another type of miracle (defined as "miracle is a correction" (*A Course in Miracles*, 1996) that frequently occurs within the breath is the experience of a past life. Many times, people report that they have an experience of being someone else in another time. They will say, "It was me. I was a gypsy dancing around a fire." They describe being in a tomb in Egypt, or being on the plains as an Indian. One of the most remarkable past life stories I ever heard was from a young man who experienced himself as an aborigine. It was the first time he had ever attended a Cellular Theta Breathing class. He experienced an entire event from what he felt was a past life, within that one session. This event was not one of the happier ones, but it was memorable in detail and in his belief that it explained why he had certain issues today. You see, the breath is not always pleasant, but it can change your life and your perceptions. Although painful, the dream is telling this young man something about loss and life, about the way he believes, about prejudice, and about how he can heal himself. It is an experience that will continue to give him meaning over and over, as he relives it.

I have traveled to many times and places in the breath sessions. Do we make up the past life experiences and premonitions when this happens in these sessions? It is possible. But the better question is: what purpose can these experiences play in your life, if any? I have personally had the pleasure of permanently releasing some of my fear in life. One time, I had a past life regression in which I entered the body of a woman being stabbed to death. By entered, I mean that I was her. I entered like this. I find myself in a void very much like being in a thick soupy fog. I can only see that surrounding me in a circle are dark circles, tunnels, and I feel that I can enter into any that I choose. As I am thinking about a woman that I have felt myself be many times before, a redheaded woman in a long green dress standing on a hill overlooking a castle, I am drawn into a tunnel that leads into her body, with a sword piercing her side. She is dying, but I am moving backward through time and space.

With this experience, actually I no longer have as much fear as before. The enormous amounts of fear and anxiety I have had in this life have been a driving force for me to find peace. The fact that I was moving away from her death because the event was going backwards made me realize how traumatized my cells would be from this event. And yet, at the same time, the total revelation reverberates throughout my body that the event is actually fleeting rather than permanent. It is as if the cells freeze fear within their memories when trauma occurs.

In your current life, the mind and body will do exactly the same thing with traumas. The event freezes fear linked with a memory of all the content of the event, including your breath pattern at the time. Then, you are constantly waiting for the event to occur again. The same breath pattern can trigger it. The same odor, color, space, or symbolic content can re-trigger you. You are hyper-vigilant, on alert, waiting to experience the trauma again and again. Breath techniques can release your need to be hyper-vigilant. The breath can release fear. This red-haired woman is the subject of her own book in this future life.

By seeing how fleeting the stabbing death is, and by noticing that I am around to observe the death adds up to one rather weird dream. The experience of my own death transforms in my mind and my fear releases. This transformation is similar to experiences described by people who have had near-death experiences. They are no longer afraid of death because they experience that death is an illusion. Fear is an adrenaline-fueled illusion. It is real in the sense that pumping adrenaline is unpleasant. It is real in the sense that pain can be intolerable. But at the point that you leave your body, these sensations are gone. If the sensation is gone and you are still present, then the awful quality disappears. You are left with a question of who are you when you are not your sensations.

Although you can release fear with Cellular Theta Breathing, it is not really as intensely emotionally activating as rebirthing. It is a slower, more nurturing route to releasing psychological material. Even these seemingly painful breath sessions are slowly released and processed over time, and because you are dreaming, it is as if you maintain some emotional distance or safety. Because the reality slows down and you have epiphanies, this technique can be a light speed route to enlightenment. You can increase these benefits by adding this breathing method to any meditative process such as yoga, tai chi, qigong, etc., that you currently use.

Some really pleasant miracles can occur in theta breathing. You can see angels or other saintly appearing beings in long robes. Stairs sometimes appear, or a tunnel of light leading to blissful states of peace. Although the mind questions the tunnel or the appearance of stairs, the compulsion to enter the tunnel or climb the stairs often overwhelms the fear of the mind. Walking up the stairs, one has little or no conscious idea about what is at the top of the stairs. When you climb them, you may find yourself floating, or you may feel that the walk is effortless. The climb may seem to take a second or could feel like hours. Intense emotions actually stop the visions from occurring within the breath. If you are thinking, "Wow, look at that," the vision evaporates. To see the vision, one must hold the mind still! Practicing trains the mind to be still. In other words, learn to observe without emotionally reacting, or you may push away the vision.

Cellular Theta Breathing has been called an ascension experience! Ascension is not permanent in this case, at least not for me. I am still on Earth when the breath is over. But you can easily understand why it is called an ascension experience when it appears to take you to another level of awareness, or to perhaps another dimension full of advanced beings. If you are visiting angels and advanced beings in long robes, it feels like you are in consciousness, ascended!

It is said that the breath raises your frequency. What does that mean? Literally, it would mean that you are vibrating at a quicker rate. Your brainwave slows down as the vibration of your atoms change frequency. Is this in fact true, I don't know? You don't see the movement of your atoms. You are unaware of the vibration of the planet, or even the pulse of your brain. You may be aware of the beating of your heart, but most of the time you are too busy to notice. When you change your frequency, it means that you could disappear from the sight of others because your frequency moves at a rate that is out of view. You don't cease to exist, but instead, you move into another dimension. While in the theta state, you are intentionally visiting another frequency.

Have I seen anyone disappear? No I have not. However, I have been told, and told more than once by more than one person that I have disappeared in the breath. One time, I was in a hallway in my office, but I was also in another room full of angels. Two staff members said that I was gone! I don't know. The event felt exactly like any other breath session to me. The only thing I was doing differently was that I was chanting a few ancient names for God as well as fasting, as I was engaged in a breath session. We will be talking more about chanting later on. Please don't come over to my office with a camera because disappearing is not important. Peace of mind, love, and compassion are what is important. I don't practice or teach disappearing. I practice peace and the peaceful creation of destiny.

After you have been practicing this breath technique for a while, people will ask you what you have done to yourself. They will think that you are wearing makeup to make your skin glow! Or they will think that you had a face-lift. If you do the breath every day, it becomes very noticeable! And you feel very peaceful because your fear diminishes and diminishes, even if your breath sessions have nothing to do with fear. It is tension, stress or anxiety that is being profoundly relieved. People will wonder why you look happier or more radiant than others do. You will be getting more oxygen than most people are obtaining with the normal shallow stressed out breath of busy daily life.

You could have unpleasant visions in the breath. As you have seen, I have had a few, and have heard of a few. They are not as common as the other types of experiences, but they do happen. Most people would say that being in the body of a woman being stabbed in the sad life of despair was awful. However, it wasn't awful to me. To me, the dreams feel like an education for your soul. Your dreams can mirror your consciousness. Dreams will help you to process conflicts from your daily life that you may not even remember having. If you have lots of garbage in your trash can, you will have lots of trash to empty. But once empty, you will find the peace that exists in the void. Underneath a layer of negative emotions, you find pure love.

One breath experience that I did perceive as awful was a session in which I saw so many horrible events during the breath that I thought I would be traumatized when I awoke. It was as if I saw all the pain and suffering of the entire world, past and present, in a flash. But before the breath ended, I expanded out until I was as large as the universe. All the pain and suffering became a speck of reality, like a grain of sand compared to the ocean of existence. When I awoke, the people around me didn't exactly like how it felt to be around me when I had the experience in the breath, but afterwards, I felt transformed. It reminds me of the saying, making a mountain out of a molehill. Isn't life so much like that? We are often so concerned with our little problems and about not getting our way that we forget to be grateful for the big picture, for our abundant blessings. Focusing on the whole often puts negativity in perspective.

The reason the staff would feel my negative experience is because the facilitators are working with the energy of the participants in the beginning of every breath session, checking their progress and helping with the breath patterns. When standing over someone having intense dreams, the facilitators tune into the energy. Needless to say, a person having intense negativity or suffering is not pleasant to be around at that point. To understand suffering and compassion from an intellectual point of view is only one level. Cellular Theta Breathing provides an opportunity to experience it from another level; perhaps from the perspective in which we are truly connected to the experience as part of the greater reality.

Remember that the breathing sessions occur in a sequence, and each one is unique to each individual. You seem to have the experience in the breath that you need that day. And many experiences are beyond description. Words cannot describe the beauty you may witness or the love you can encounter.

I have been in a room full of loving angels, surrounded by them, and feeling unconditional love emanating from all of them. That experience was more intense than the vision with the pain and suffering, because the feeling of love from thousands of angels was indescribably intense. The pain and suffering experiences are easier to describe! Do you think that perhaps we have an easier time being negative than positive? I believe that the mind is naturally more obsessed with what is wrong since that could be perceived as a threat. Why should the mind naturally be interested in what is right, what is good, unless you intentionally focus your attention in that direction. Focus on what is positive in your world. Focus on what you would think this life would be like if it were heavenly, and create that life now.

It could be difficult to accept heavenly. When I have received enormous amounts of angelic love in the breath, I can tell you how I felt. I cried. I felt unworthy. I felt my heart expanding and opening so much, I thought it would burst. I thought it was a mistake. I tried to tell the angels that they must have me mistaken for someone else. They told me that I am honored. They told me that they honor everyone on this planet. They love us much more than we love ourselves, and many of us do not love ourselves at all, which troubles them. They said that they have no perception of how we couldn't love ourselves because they love us so much. That is the vision and feeling that I can describe, a description that is inadequate.

I have also seen saints sitting in a large room along with other beings in long robes. Several of them will greet me, and proceed to give me instructions. I am always telling them that I don't feel worthy of this attention. They are patient with me and continue giving me instructions. They seem to give the same instructions over and over in one session, as if I will forget. They are right. Later, these instructions, like a dream, can immediately become hazy or disappear from conscious awareness when you wake. You will remember your dreams better if you journal immediately upon awakening.

Many describe the time in a breath experience much like your life flashing in front of you when you die, similar to the way in which people describe near-death experiences. It is as if you live a lifetime in a few minutes, a saga in a second or two.

Time, sound, and feelings alter. A tiny puff of air feels like a fan blowing on your face. A barking dog next to your ear makes no entrance into your thoughts, but an infinitely small noise sounds like thunder. A small pain intensifies, or all pain disappears instantly.

Are all of these visions a fantasy? I don't know. I do know that those who continually do Cellular Theta Breathing clear issues in their life. They get over psychological blocks. However, to keep doing the breath regularly is not easy. As with any practice, the mind likes to forget about practicing breath, just like forgetting something good for you, like going to the gym. The mind can really fight this process because it is usually very attached to the reality of old and seemingly sacred beliefs.

In therapy, you attempt to unlock the reality of beliefs and expand the possibility for the mind. In Cellular Theta Breathing, this expansion continues and continues. All you have to do is practice it on a regular basis to progress.

The only danger in the breathing is addiction! Can you believe it? Of course people can make Cellular Theta Breathing their god, just as they could make smoking, drinking, exercise, dieting, gambling, spending, sex, religion, etc. a god. If you are seeing angels in the breath sessions, you might miss the point and think the point is to see angels. No, the point is to decrease fear and increase love. If you are swooned by Cellular Theta Breathing, then you are missing the point!

> *"It doesn't matter how wonderful or uplifting your experience was; you turn from that and go on to the next thing. To do less is to deny your growth and awareness."*
>
> –John-Roger
> (From: The Tao of Spirit)

OK, you have been told how you do the breathing. You definitely need a facilitator to teach you, just as you do with rebirthing. However, you don't necessarily need a therapist because this breath technique is much more gentle that rebirthing. A Breath Facilitator will actually breathe with you and work with your energy field. After you learn this technique, you can practice it on your own, but you are not trained to facilitate others. If you facilitate others, you will work with their energy. Most of us cannot even work with our own energy, much less someone else's.

What is an energy field? Imagine that is looks like a donut of magnetic energy surrounding your body, maybe looking like luminous fibers. This energy or light field is sometimes called the etheric body. It is invisible to most people, although some people say that they can see it. Some say that they can sense it or feel its presence. Some call it the aura. Some distinguish between the aura and the etheric body. Let us say it is energy that belongs to you. Within this field are energy centers called chakras. These chakras are like vortexes of energy swirling in a clockwise fashion over different areas of your body. Each energy center has particular influences on the body (Myss, 1996). During a breath session, a facilitator senses this energy and works with you to unblock your energy flow if it is blocked in any way. If you study the chakra centers and work on this energy, you could help to heal your body, mind, and/or soul.

At the beginning of a breath session, you are in a comfortable position, having water close by, blankets, pillows, or whatever you will require for comfort. The breath session lasts for about one hour, in addition to a half-hour for instruction and another half-hour for talking about the breath session afterwards. The lights are dim and candles are lit. Music accompanies the session, and determines the length of the session. Music that is conducive to the theta state would be relaxing, mostly instrumental. Any words in your music will influence your journey. Two of the pieces of music we use most frequently are *Novus Magnificat* by Constance Demby, and *Mystical Traveler* by Chris Spheeris. *Novus Magnificat* is used for first-time participants, and *Mystical Traveler* for advanced participants. *Novus* is fully instrumental and *Mystical Traveler* contains chanting along with beautiful music. A second piece of music by Constance Demby, *Aeterna* is also a favorite.

As the music begins, the breathing begins. Recall that the breath pattern is a deep breath, which is like you are taking two breaths, and travels from the base of your spine all the way up and though all your chakras or energy centers. Imagine your breath traveling the entire length of the spine until you are about twelve inches above your head. When your inhale reaches your throat, tilt your head back a little to increase the flow of oxygen as you take what amounts to a second inhale. The jaw is relaxed. Your exhale will be a sigh, which you will imagine is flowing from your heart. Continue taking these deep breaths for approximately five minutes. Almost immediately with the first or second breath, you may feel tingling in your face, hands, and maybe feet. Your mind could tell you to stop in various ways. Keep breathing. The breathing doesn't harm you. A little extra oxygen is good for you. Could you get excessive, yes, but the body will probably not allow it! You may have to fight the body and mind to breathe this way for a few minutes. If you are one of the rare people who think that if five minutes is good, twenty minutes will be better, you are wrong. The point of the breathing is to enter the theta brainwave, not to get obsessive about air! When you enter theta, it often feels like a wave pulling you into a deep state of relaxation, although your mind may keep chattering away at the same time. Do **not** keep deep breathing until you enter theta. Breathe deeply for five or ten minutes and stop naturally. More and more breathing may be you trying to control yourself into a state, which creates tension rather than dreaming. Stop the deep breathing and listen to the music for a while. The breath in connection to releasing control and flowing are the elements of theta. Sometimes, you lose track of time and the music. Sometimes, you get a cramp or pain in your body. That sensation may be blocked energy. If you send some more air and imagine some white light flowing into that sensation, it will release. If you clamp down on the pain, it will intensify. Imagine it is like a tightly held fist. Move your consciousness to the fist, and slowly release it, gently nudging it open with the breathing, and with your consciousness.

The facilitators breathe along with participants, forming a type of bond. The prayer stated at the beginning of the breath session is to ask for spiritual help from angels, guides, your higher self or higher power, and to set a healing intention. Protection is requested, and for the highest good to be produced within the breath session. In other words, the facilitators don't know how to heal anyone; we only know how to help you heal yourself. Your higher self can heal you, and we ask for that to happen. We are not defining your higher power as we are being respectful of each person's personal spiritual belief.

You will often feel energy emanating from the facilitator's hands, some more than others. The facilitators are consciously pulling in energy through their hearts and the tops of their heads, and releasing it out of their hands, which they then give to the participants. People often have complete relief of pain when touched by a facilitator. Participants will also often go into the theta state in the presence, or by the touch of a facilitator because the brainwave state is contagious. Breath facilitators are people who offer love and compassion to others. They are healers. They practice the breath regularly, study many forms of healing, are deeply spiritual, and continue always with their own personal growth.

When you are in theta, the facilitators get there first. The breath session continues until the music ends. You flow between the states of mind from beta to alpha to theta to delta. You flow back and forth between brainwave states throughout the session. At the end, the facilitators will tell you to take a deep breath and slowly come back. A drink of water is offered to the participant. The breathing can give you a dry mouth, and the body releases toxins which water helps to flush out of the body.

At a class, a discussion follows. At the retreat, a discussion is done in terms of journal writing. You write about your experience and about your mind talk. If you are with a therapist, as is the case in our classes, we may interpret a dream for you. But this interpretation is unnecessary. The dream is the experience that talks to you about your conflicts with life. The interpretation is often just for fun and conversation. The primary reason we have the discussion is to be fully awake to drive home, as well as to remember the material.

Cellular Theta Breathing in a group session is different from individual sessions. Within the group, all the participants contribute to a group energy, which each individual may feel. For example, if many in the group have very deep theta experiences, it may help newcomers to enter the theta state more readily. At a retreat, you will have a theta state of consciousness developing over and over for several days. This intensified theta state takes place away from your normal life, and you will experience the world from an increasingly expanded state of consciousness. You can now observe a world that you have forgotten to notice. The natural world ceases to exist when you run through your daily life in the more rapidly pulsing beta state.

Individual sessions have all the benefits of one-on-one care. The facilitator has undivided attention on your experience and energy. If your desire is physical, emotional, and mental healing, the individual session will be more of an intensive experience.

Cellular Theta Breathing is a powerful tool for healing and for raising your frequency quickly! Are you ready to become lighter than you have ever been? Are you ready to have more oxygen? All you need to do is move beyond the rigidity of the mind's survival mode and into the breath.

"Take a deep breath." The voice sounds like it is coming from a distance but actually is the facilitator speaking to the participants. The music has stopped. "I would like you to take a short break, in silence, for water, bathroom, and come back for another meditation.

'Whoa, I feel tired.' Deanna feels almost like she needs to go back to sleep again. 'How can I need sleep? I have been doing nothing but sleeping, eating, and writing since I got here. Am I this tired? I must have been so stressed out that I didn't realize it. I am so glad we are going to go right back under so I can just rest some more.'

Melanie is writing in her journal even though she wasn't instructed to. 'That was some dream.' She is so moved by it that she can barely stand to do anything but write about Matthew. 'I cannot wait to tell Jack about Matthew.' She is afraid she won't remember her dream if she doesn't write about it right now. She is excited to write about the son she encountered, and wants to share this dream with her husband Jack when she returns home. 'That breath meditation made me feel so tired and drained.' She sinks back into her covers, feeling strange. 'That is all I need. I come here for peace and relaxation and come down with something that will ruin the rest of my retreat.' Melanie quickly reverts to her negative thinking with a tinge of tiredness. Melanie's mind moves from elation to irritation within a millisecond.

Just then, the break ends and the music begins again, for the next meditation.

Destiny
(© Diane Donovan-Vaughn, 1996)

"Close your eyes. Take deep connected breaths. Pay attention to your breath and with each breath, go deeper and deeper and deeper inside. Let your thoughts flow through you, like a meandering stream, peacefully passing by.

"Imagine that a pillar of brilliant golden white light is entering through the top of your head and washing away any tension that you may be holding within your body. Feel the light flowing through your body, like a river bathing all the cells of your body, soothing you and taking you deeper and deeper and deeper.

"As the tension fades away, you become lighter and lighter and lighter. You feel more and more comfortable. As you breathe in, you breathe in the light. As you breathe out, you continue releasing any tensions and problems. Breathe in the light. Breathe out the tension.

"The golden white light begins to remind you of a far-away memory of a place that you have been to sometime before. This far-away place is beyond your conscious mind, somewhere deep within you. You long to go there, but in the longing, you feel some tension returning. Breathe in the light and breathe out the tension. Relax and begin to imagine the far-away place. You may find this place by relaxing and allowing the memory to flow in, like the river of light flowing through you. Relax and remember the long-ago forgotten place of light.

"You find yourself standing beyond the clouds, beyond tunnels of brilliant pink iridescent light, in a place of indescribable peace and love. Gaze at the iridescent colors of pink, pearl, silver, gold, and white. The many brilliant hues are familiar and wondrous. You look around and know you are at home here, as you are surrounded in these colors and enfolded

in love. The love here is familiar. You are filled with love, compassion, and peace. As you bask in this peaceful love, you hear beautiful music playing all around you. It is both comforting and inspiring.

"You find yourself thinking about the colors in the clouds of a sunset, and as you do, you become aware of your ability to transform the scene in an instant of thought into another place. You are not aware of traveling, but the scene transforms into clouds, and the many cloud colors of a gorgeous sunset. How, you wonder can you transform a scene with just your thought? But you have a deeper knowing of your creative ability in this place of light.

"As you ponder your creative ability, you think a new thought of the times you have seen the clouds setting behind mountains. Instantly, you find yourself in a meadow in the mountains, with deep shades of greens and many colorful wildflowers. You hear the sounds of the forest and smell the fragrance of the meadow. This meadow is peaceful and you continue to feel the love surrounding you. You are so relaxed and carefree here. Sit down among the flowers and breathe in the fragrance of the meadow. Ah, such beauty!

"Full of beautiful sights and smells, your mind wanders to the thought of the ocean, and instantly another transformation occurs. Now you find yourself at the beach. Once again, you are not aware of traveling, but the environment has changed. You have a strong urge to touch the water. Reach down and brush the cool ocean water with your hand. Lift your hand to your mouth and taste the salty water. Yes, it tastes like the ocean. The sounds of water and seagulls fill your ears. The gulls are calling overhead in a rhythm with the crashing waves. Beneath your feet warm, sand tickles your skin enticing you to sit. Gaze out across the water and notice the sun sparkling on the water. The horizon beckons you, and you notice the sunset again. The colors remind *you of the place of beautiful colors, and once again you find yourself in the place of light.*

"What is this place of light and love that transforms with a thought? You know you have been here before. From this light place, everything is clear. The creative possibilities of lifetimes and many journeys are here. It is here that you are preparing to embark on a great journey. The path of this journey is being planned now. You will be entering through a tunnel of light into the life of your creation. You have a mission, a goal, and you are determined to be successful as you view the possibilities for this upcoming adventure into humanity.

"In your preparation, you must carefully pick the path that may lead you to your mission. You know that the path may also stop you cold; forever destroying your will to go on. You know the temptation to quit will be with you. The path is like a tightrope, one step in either direction off the path and you may fall. You take as much light and knowledge as you can gather to help remind yourself of your extremely important mission. Even though the path is narrow for success, you feel optimistic.

"You ask yourself, "Do I have enough reminders to keep me from quitting and losing my way... from forgetting my mission?"

"As you think about the reminders, all of the other people who are to be with you on this path appear in an instant. You recognize them; all the many players on the path with you. As they appear, you confer with them. The love among you is all-encompassing, surrounding you, and fulfilling you. You are all connected as one in person, mission, and love.

"The oneness is like the beautiful, iridescent light, all-knowing, and in harmony. Complete agreement exists among you, and many signs are given for recognition of each other. A certain smile and a certain name will remind you later that these people are on your path.

"You feel ready now. Your life is chosen... the one life for

your mission... the life that will motivate you to your life purpose as well as discourage you from completing your goal, the tightrope path.

"In front of you, a tunnel of white light appears. Step toward the tunnel and pause before you depart; pulling into yourself as much knowledge as possible, hoping that you can maintain enough memory to keep you on your path. Remember... Remember the others...

"Remember the path...

"Remember the mission...

"This life is preparing you for your destiny... your destiny is love.

"Remember the purpose. This life is leading you to your mission. Whatever happens to you is to prepare you for your mission.

"Remember your destiny... your destiny is love.

"Now, allow yourself to flow into the tunnel of light. Feel yourself being drawn at high speed through time and space. See billions of lines, and pull some of the lines along with you that you know are more of the knowledge... the knowledge that you will be able to remember if you listen.

"You travel to your destination... your destiny... and light starts changing as you prepare to arrive. Now, it is brilliant white light.

"You arrive in some confusion and you are unable to convey any of your experiences to those around you. You are filled with emotions. As time passes, the light place becomes foggy, just beyond your memory. You are a bundle of physical and emotional feelings, more concerned with your feelings, and with your survival.

"As the mind learns to think, you start explaining life with the mind. You feel lost but you don't know why. You are wandering aimlessly among other lost people. Sometimes, you *feel like you can explain everything, but you have forgotten why you are here. You are wondering... "Why am I here?" But the question is uncomfortable. What is this situation called life in which I find myself mired? This stuck place is a roadblock. You are looking at a roadblock. For most of your life, your roadblock is what you think life is about. You try to work through it, get over it, accept it, forgive it, worship it, make it your career, or spouse. You think your roadblock is the most important thing in your life. You are embracing it, ignoring it, or running from it, but the roadblock runs your life.*

"You are spending your life in response to your roadblock.

"Stop, and ask yourself now:

"What is the purpose of this roadblock?"

"What is the purpose of this roadblock?"

"Now, consider this question... If my roadblock is like a college education for my mission, then what degree will I receive if I graduate? And if I graduate and move beyond my roadblock, what will I be doing? What is my next step, my path in life, my destiny?

"What has my roadblock been teaching me?

"Thank your roadblock for the fantastic lessons you have learned.

"Look at these lessons carefully, for within them is a life review.

"Watch as your life flashes before you in a review. Look at your life like a painting, reviewing it carefully for the overall picture. Your whole life in this review of your lessons is the training that you have been receiving in order to accomplish your next step... your destiny.

"You are multifaceted like a beautiful diamond in the rough, being polished by your life. You are everything that has occurred before in your life, a culmination of events... wonderful, horrible, and mundane. Every event has shaped you and molded *you, until you are here at this very moment looking at your destiny.*

"Move to your heart and feel it awaken and open with the key of your mission. Feel your heart expand as you breathe in the purpose of your life. This realization is what you have been seeking outside of yourself, without success. Now, your heart's desire is being found at last.

"Find yourself standing among iridescent clouds, beyond tunnels of pink light in a place beyond description, a place of iridescent colors of pink, pearl, silver, gold, and white... many hues of white and gold. You are bathed in these colors, and surrounded in love, compassion, and peace.

"In this place, you experience yourself as your higher purpose. Ask yourself, "What is my destiny? What is my higher purpose, my mission of love and light?"

"Answer yourself; "I am ready to move beyond my roadblocks into my destiny and into a state of grace. I am prepared to accomplish my goals, to acknowledge my friends who are with me on this path. Together, we will accomplish this great goal, the mission that is our destiny of love, compassion, and peace. Feel the oneness you have with all others in this focus of love and compassion.

"Who are they? The people in your life... who are they? As you remember them... who are they? See them appearing in your mind... and remember the signs... Remember what you are here to do together... Remember ...

"You are returning to your body with the feeling of oneness and love in your heart. Remember your destiny. Take a deep breath, and breathe in the colors and the peace as you are returning to your body."

When the meditation draws to a close, the facilitator asks the participants to begin writing in their journals about their breath experience, and the meditation. They settle down to the task accompanied by the ever softly playing music, while quietly recording everything they can about their experiences before breaking for lunch. The facilitators advise them to return prepared for an outdoor activity.

Chapter Seven Journal Questions

1. How is your breathing most of the time?
2. What happens to your breathing throughout your day?
3. What in your life can make your breathing shallow?
4. How does deep breathing affect you?
5. What issues would you like to alter?
6. How could relaxation and breathing change your life?
7. What do you think your life has been teaching you so far?
8. Who are the important people in your life, and what have they been teaching you?
9. What is your destiny in this life?

Chapter 8 I Am the Element

"Above all else I want to see things differently."
   —*A Course in Miracles, 1975*

"Climb the mountains and get their good tidings. Nature's peace will flow into you as sunshine flows into trees. The winds will blow their own freshness into you, and the storms their energy, while cares will drop away from you like the leaves of autumn."
   —John Muir (1838 - 1914)

"The goal of life is living in agreement with nature."
—Zeno (335 BC - 264 BC), from Diogenes Laertius, Lives of Eminent Philosophers

    Deanna and Melanie look like longtime friends as they walk together back from lunch in silence. They are actually rather good at following the rules about being quiet and staying together. In fact, the energy between them is now very cordial and friendly after the rough start they had in the beginning. Both of them look more relaxed and healthy after all the meditation and breathing of the morning, although Melanie is still ruminating about being tired. 'How can I be tired with all this resting going on? Maybe Deanna's sleepiness is catching. Ha! Boy, this listening to your mind talk makes me feel crazy. I never realized how much garbage my mind goes on about. I guess it is always droning on like this, but am I always so negative?'

Mother and daughter, Sophia and Madison, are separated. Madison is off wandering around, checking out the pool on the grounds, while her mother is reading in their room. They didn't eat together and neither did they stay together as directed. Plus, Sophia has trouble being on time, which is frustrating her daughter, and always has. Madison doesn't talk about it because she is following the rules, but her mother continually breaks the rules in a complete role reversal, with Madison feeling like she is the parent of the teenager on this retreat. 'I just don't get how she did this retreat the first time. She must just be disrespecting me and treated a stranger better than me!' See, although Madison appears to be exploring the site, she is really getting some distance from her mother, and moping about how she is being treated. She is depressed about the treatment, and her mind is playing tricks on her. Will she notice that this is what is called mind talk to be recorded, or will she just go on believing what is happening without notation?

Further back on the path, holding hands are Susan and Darryl. Susan is the image of happiness, spending all this quality time alone with Darryl, and he is in heaven because they can be together in nature without interruptions. They are really having a good time.

As the participants enter the room, they are prepared for an outside activity as requested, but first they must settle back into their sleeping bags for a meditation in preparation for a hike. As they assume their individual meditation positions, the music changes and a voice begins…

I am the Element
(©Diane Donovan-Vaughn, 1996)

"Close your eyes. Breathe and become one with your breath, breathing in and out with small mystical pauses of breathlessness interspersed evenly and rhythmically in each cycle of breath.

"Allow your consciousness to become of aware of your toes. Be at one with your toes. As you are at one with your toes, let the knowledge of the cells of your toes be your knowing. What do your cells say when they speak? LISTEN! (Pause)

"Now, let your consciousness expand to encompass your feet. Be at one with your feet. As you are at one with your feet, let the knowledge of the cells of your feet be your knowing. What do your cells say when they speak? LISTEN! (Pause)

"Now, let your consciousness expand to encompass your legs. Be at one with your legs. As you are at one with your legs, let the knowledge of the cells of your legs be your knowing. What do your cells say when they speak? LISTEN! (Pause)

"Now, let your consciousness expand to encompass the trunk of your body. Be at one with the trunk of your body. As you are at one with the trunk of your body, let the knowledge of the cells of the trunk of your body be your knowing. What do your cells say when they speak? LISTEN! (Pause)

"Now, let your consciousness expand to encompass your arms. Be at one with your arms. As you are at one with your arms, let the knowledge of the cells of your arms be your knowing. What do your cells say when they speak? LISTEN! (Pause)

"Now, let your consciousness expand once again to encompass your neck and head. Be at one with your neck and head. As you are at one with your neck and head, let the

knowledge of the cells of your neck and head be your knowing. What do your cells say when they speak? LISTEN! (Pause)

"Notice that you are now at one with your whole body. Let your consciousness become aware of every cell in your whole body. Be at one with each and every one of your cells. As you are at one with all of your cells, let their knowledge become your knowing. What do your cells say when they speak? LISTEN! (Pause)

"Now take several deep breaths. As you breathe, breathe in your newfound wholeness. In this instant, feel the integration of your whole being. You are now one with every cell of your body. Keep breathing. As you are breathing, notice a golden white light above you and all around you. Breathe in the white light. Immerse every cell in the white light. Expand your consciousness to the subatomic level of your being. Allow your consciousness to become aware that you are now space, and you are now light. You are now in a creative state of peaceful, loving space and light. All of your atoms have joined together to create your cells. All your cells have joined together to create your body. Simultaneously, all of your joining and creating is occurring according to your will, according to your plan. You are space and light... moving particles or waves of light.

"Now, as your awareness is at a level of space and light, let your consciousness expand again to encompass the space and light around you. Remember, you are at one with everything that your consciousness encompasses; the chair or the floor beneath you, the air surrounding you that you are breathing and sharing with others around you. All of the atoms in all creation are space and moving particles or waves of light.

"Allow yourself to be pure consciousness, now expanding your awareness out and becoming one with the environment surrounding your body consciousness. Let the knowing of these areas become your knowing. What do these areas of space and

light say when they speak? LISTEN! (Pause)

"As you continue breathing rhythmically, slowly expand out even farther to encompass the other bodies close to you, along with the air and space around all of you. Notice how the feeling of separation disappears among you as you become one large area of space and light. Feel the peacefulness fall upon you as you expand into this awareness. Let their knowing become your knowing. What do these peaceful areas of space and light say when they speak? LISTEN! (Pause)

"Once again, keep expanding your consciousness. Expand out to encompass the whole room and everything in it. Become one with the room. Let the knowing of the room become your knowing. What does this area of space and light say when it speaks? LISTEN! (Pause)

"Now, expand your consciousness again, even farther this time. Expand outside this room to the whole retreat area of space and light. Become one with all the messages you are receiving and learning... one with all the people here... one with all the nature around you. Become one with everything in this area. What do all these areas of space and light say when they speak? LISTEN! (Pause)

"Breathe in the oneness and allow your expanded consciousness to flow outside of this area, and into the larger countryside. Keep expanding across the state. Keep expanding farther and farther and farther and farther. EXPAND! KEEP EXPANDING AND EXPANDING! Remember to become one with everything you come in contact with... all of creation. You are expanding your whole being across the entire Earth. You can now feel the entire Earth as your whole consciousness as you encircle it and encompass it. As your consciousness integrates with all creation on the planet... know that you are being given a very precious gift. You are being given the gift of all the energy of space and light of each creation that you unite

with. You now have a newfound appreciation for all that is the planet Earth. You are all of Earth, and all of Earth is you. What do all the areas of space and light of the Earth say when they speak? LISTEN! (Pause)

"Now that you have expanded across the planet, it is time to expand even farther. It is time to expand your consciousness to the outer limits of all time and space. Take a DEEP breath! Take another deep breath, and as you exhale, feel yourself expanding throughout the entire solar system, encompassing all the planets and moons and space. Keep expanding and move beyond the solar system to the stars, their planets, moons, and to all being. See your consciousness glowing with the white light and spreading out across the infinity of space... becoming one with everything in the universe, spreading out as the universe spreads out on its ever-expanding quest. What do all the areas of space and light in the universe say when they speak? LISTEN! (Pause)

"When you feel you have expanded your consciousness to infinity, stop for a moment and just be. You are pure being, one with everything. Feel the unlimited potential in this state of being. Breathe in this blissful state of being. LISTEN! (Pause)

"Now, you are ready to begin your journey back... bringing with you all the energy within all the light and space of the universe, bringing with you all the knowledge and energy of pure being.

"As you begin your journey back, be aware of all your senses. Open up all your senses and experience everything that you have become one with. Now that you have taken on the energy of, and become one with all existence, you will experience your senses at a much more vivid and evolved level. As you journey back to Earth, look at the expansion of beautiful colors of the planet. You are now seeing them with a much more vivid focus. Look at all the different hues of red, orange, yellow, green, blue, and purple. Experience and enjoy all these colors in

a new way, as you have never seen them before. What do these colors say when they speak? LISTEN! (Pause)

"As you reach the planet, touch the water. Experience a whole new sensation of the refreshing coolness as it moistens your skin. Feel the planet with your expanded sense of touch. What does your touch say it when it feels in this new expanded way? LISTEN! (Pause)

"Now, lie down very still in the grass, feeling the softness against your skin and listen to the vivid sounds of Mother Earth and all her creations as she sings... the whistle of the wind, the chirping of the birds, the buzzing and snapping of little insects that you have never heard before, the crashing of the ocean, the peacefulness of the sky, and the rumbling of the ground as it settles. What do the vibrations of the sounds say when they speak? LISTEN! (Pause)

"Now, walk through the orchards and fields and enjoy your new sensation of taste as you bite into the fruits and vegetables that Mother Earth has given to you. Taste the juices and natural flavors as you have never experienced before. What do your new tastes say when they speak? LISTEN! (Pause)

"Now experience one last expanded sense, the sense of smell. Walk through flower gardens with your new sense of smell, and experience the blissful aroma of Mother Earth. What do these smells say when they speak? LISTEN! (Pause)

"You have experienced your new senses and awareness created by the energy of all the space and light that you have become one with, and you are ready to continue your journey back. As you do this... take a deep breath and remember all that you have allowed your consciousness to experience, to encompass, and to become one with... from your toes to your head, to the other people in the room, to the places and individuals outside the room, to the wind and ocean, insects and trees, to the fruits and vegetables and orchards and fields, to the

sky, to the planets, the stars and the universes... to infinity.

"While remaining in this oneness, begin to come back into the room and back into your body, letting the knowledge of all that you have become one with, be your knowing. What do the space and light of all this oneness have to say when it speaks? LISTEN!"

As you gaze out into the world, what do you see? The programming of the mind is marching forth from birth to structure your reality into categories. The brain has done a good job of funneling through the wealth of information, and now you are dismissing great chunks of reality. As you expand your consciousness with meditations, awareness arises of ignored realities, new energies appear, and you may be surprised or even overwhelmed by the massive existence of what your mind has been dismissing.

Keep looking again and again at something that you are experiencing every day, but not really noticing anymore, like the route to work. Watch the traffic you are traversing every day of your life. Observe your thoughts and your emotions more and more deeply. What is happening to you when you are outside? Where are you going every day, and what is your purpose in going that way? Nature and the greater reality are accompanying your journeys. Can you sense it, hear it, and see it?

Now, look again, and look around at the world that you are filtering away from your view. What are you missing? People say that they are bored if not constantly stimulated. Did you ever stop and think about what constant stimulation means? What if you turn off the television, radio, computer, phones, and any other artificial stimulation? You will be left with only your environment and yourself. Listen. You can still hear the noises of the world going on around you that you don't notice anymore unless it were to stop; noises like traffic outside, planes overhead, machinery, animals, and people. Does it make you uncomfortable to be alone with yourself and nature? Are you in your house? Are you at work? What are you thinking? What emotions are you having? What are you feeling? How much artificial stimulation do you have going on in your life? How much is going on that you are unconsciously ignoring, and then when you notice it, what does your mind tell you?

The radio talks to you while you drive. The television drones on in the background. The phones ring constantly, now following you wherever you go. What if you turn them all off and listen to nature? Nature, the whole of the universe, the underlying energy of which we are all a part, that which some call God is communicating at all times. When you don't hear the voice of God, then it is because you are not listening.

When you eat, talk, sleep, and with every activity, you could be missing so much that it could take a lifetime to really contact everything in one room of your life. How can you be bored when you are unable to take it all in? But you may find that you are uncomfortable being with yourself and nature. You may be uncomfortable with the immensity of the reality in which you swim if you were aware. Breathe and relax. Listen and observe. What is the universe communicating?

When a depressed person comes into my office at work, I am watching for what they are missing. I don't have to wonder about whether their mind is lying to them when it is making their experiences awful, because it is already known to me that the mind is doing a number on them. The mind is always lying. Of course, when you are depressed, you really don't like to hear that you are being inaccurate in your assessment of reality. You believe in the awful state of your life completely. It is you in your black hole of reality, with no rungs on the sides from which to climb out of that pit of darkness.

If this person could only experience the wonder that exists

everywhere, instantaneously a cure would result. My office contains items that are filled with energy and could be quite amazing, but they fade into a background of the depressed existence. If you listen, nature will talk to you. Observe and leave behind the maze of mental distraction and categorizing. What would nature tell you? Nature could talk about peace, love and compassion!

OK, is the mind talking about the war of nature, the killing, the kill, or being killed? In our world, death is right in front of us every time we eat. Do you think if you are vegetarian that you are not killing the plant that you consume? Oh yes, you are altering the life of those around you all the time. What happens to the energy that we eat? Have you noticed the energy of the food you eat? If you stopped and observed the energy of the food when you eat it and after it enters your body, your eating habits would change. You would hear your food communicating.

So what is nature telling you? How do birds live? They don't work eight to five and drive in traffic. They don't carry a cell phone strapped to their bodies to converse with other birds. The food they find is out there in the world. A species can cease to exist on this planet because of humans all the time these days. Nature is talking to you. It is the voice of enlightenment you may be ignoring with worldly distractions. However, when you first have compassion with nature, it might cause you to feel uncomfortable!

What if you become conscious of nature? What if you are consciously grateful for every morsel that passes through your mouth that nourishes your body? What if you talk to your food? What if you talk to trees, to water, to every aspect of your life, even the components of your car? Most of the world might think you are talking to yourself, and potentially crazy, or maybe they would just think you have a Bluetooth device strapped to your ear. If you read a book about the adventures you can have when you listen to nature, they will be hard to believe. But nature can lead you to see, hear, smell, taste, and touch realities that you never dreamed possible. When you listen to nature, the lizards talk to you. Ravens point you to your destination. And your food; enlightened food is beyond what you have tasted up until now. Plus the energy of all reality continues existing even when you think it is gone.

Every second of every day, you are missing what the Earth, nature and the universe are saying to you, unless you are listening. The best part about listening is that your world expands so rapidly that you never need a distraction again, because boredom will cease to exist in your world. You are so far behind in experiencing every nuance of reality that you can never experience it all if you continue trying in a linear way. Linear thinking, which is past, present, and future lines of thinking, will cease to exist when you begin experiencing enlightenment more and more frequently. The view from a multidimensional view will allow you to see it all.

At one time, people said that enlightenment was something you had to sit on a mountain and seek for many years. You could still do it that way if you want. Or you could have a multidimensional reality, experiencing enlightenment as you go about your life. Of course, your life will be quite magical. Your life will occur in one continuous NOW.

Will you get sucked into negative limited thinking once you learn to talk to nature? Oh yes! You are a human with adrenaline, are you not? Remember what we discussed earlier that the space of time can decrease between the adrenaline we normally pump and finding peace of mind. You can have your reaction in seconds rather than hours or days! Have you ever felt like your life was put on hold because of obsessions you have had? Have you ever wished you could take back something you said or did? Have you ever wasted days being trapped in an issue; pouting, depressed, angry, and in fear? By the way, all of these reactions are about fear, but more about that later.

Moving your consciousness toward nature, away from your limited survival mode, you will find that all around you is a greater consciousness of which you are a part. You are talking to your big self when you are talking to this reality, this thing we think of as nature. It is from this expanded state of consciousness that you can find sanity. You can find your peace of mind.

The Incas talk about the spirit of the mountain and the spirit of the trees. If one didn't understand about the voice of nature, you could think that they are talking about many gods that they worship. They are actually talking to the intelligent energy that exists within all nature. The energy is in your computer. It is in your sofa. It is in your lawn and your car. This energy is the same energy that is inside of you. The Incas acknowledge the intelligence of the energy of which we are all one part. When you are in contact with nature, you are in contact with that energy. It often speaks in telepathic images or symbols. It gives direction. It is capable of being observed as good and evil, depending on the mind of the beholder. It is like an experiment with the infinitesimally tiny quark. The observer influences the outcome as if you are the creator of the result. Many of us would define miracle as being able to determine reality! Yet, if it is so, then determining our reality is actually ordinary and no miracle, but the way life really is.

Right now, you are probably unaware of, or even consciously avoiding nature. But you are affecting it with every move you make. Nature lives in you and you are nature. Breathing, you are taking in energy. Every part of you is composed of every part of everything else.

Separation ceases to exist and you become one with everything; enlightenment! Imagine if you could go through your daily life as an enlightened being, connected to everything.

What you would choose to do as an enlightened being would most likely be significantly different than what you are choosing now.

How strange to be in a world of illusion of separation when you are one with all existence. Murder would be impossible. It would be impossible to kill part of yourself. Humans try to kill off parts of the self all the time. It is impossible but still it is attempted. When you exist as a separate human, distinct from others, it seems possible to kill another. When you exist as a connected part of the whole energy, you can see that no matter what, you cannot rid yourself of another. Parts of you that you don't like, the shadow self is a part of your existence and as relevant as the parts you do like. Imagine being one with the parts of existence that you don't like or accept, accepting the parts of you that you don't like.

Talk to nature. Listen to nature. What can you hear, see, taste, smell, and touch? Then, observe beyond your ability to sense. Remember again that scientists tell us that more reality lies outside of your ability to sense. Observe again the limited nature of your life right now. You are already ignoring tons of information that you could sense through your brain's filtration system! Then there is an infinite amount of information and experience that your sensory system cannot access physically. Do you still think you need some more stimulation? Are you still able to get bored?

Be still. Until you are still, observing nature, you are disconnected.

The sparkle returns to your eyes when you are conscious of nature. You will begin to see a reality around you that you have missed. Your eyes sparkle because tears will fill them as you gaze upon beauty that is astonishing. Then, nature speaks to you in a still small voice, and with images. The clouds form a letter and the birds stop to speak to you. Nature talks to you and shows you the way. Without silence and observation, you will continue to miss the magical messages of nature. Many people have never heard nature talk. But even if you are on your computer most of the day, you could be surprised to discover that silicon makes up a great part of nature. Now, we have silicon as our communication tool! When no one is looking, have a conversation with your computer. Talk to your so-called inanimate objects. The Incas say that a rock is a very dense form of the energy you posses. You are an airy object composed of space. The rock is filled with energy. Talk to a rock. It will bring you a message. Put one up to your head and listen. It is like holding a seashell up to your ear. Have you heard the sea in a shell? What else is it saying?

A rock can guide you to an answer about a personal question in life. Why do people hug trees? Trees are full of energy, probably more than you have. If you ask a tree, it just might heal you.

Nature is the voice of the energy. Listen carefully every second of the day. It is so big and so talkative that you may begin to realize that you are enfolded and full of love. You would hear compassion, and you would hear of peace. And as for chaos, yes, chaos is part of the voice but it is not separate, it is part of the greater whole, part of the love you will feel when you listen.

Now, let's check in on the participants and see what they are hearing. Janna is joining Melanie and Deanna for their afternoon walk. No one is talking, but occasionally one of the women points to something of interest and they all react, communicating nonverbally with one another. They are doing quite well with the silence task because they are still able to communicate without words.

They are listening to nature and watching for signs as instructed by the facilitators. When one of them spots something they consider to be a coincidence or a sign, they stop in unison to appreciate the discovery. Right now, they are watching a couple of rabbits grazing on some brush in the distance.

Melanie is really shocked to discover nature because she thought she hated the outdoors. One of the reasons that she was the most reluctant about this trip concerned the location in a remote region surrounded by nothing, or so she thought before this moment. That 'nothing' is looking very appealing to her today. She is awestruck by the fullness of the landscape around her. It seems to be teeming with a life she never dreamed existed. Even the rocks and clouds seem alive.

'What has happened to me?' Melanie doesn't really understand the source or her newfound respect for her surroundings. 'That last meditation must have really been powerful because I seem to be almost... well... like... seeing the energy around the plants and rocks here.' She is feeling sort of sheepish about this discovery, like she is afraid she is losing her mind a little bit. This seeing energy around things is so weird for her, like something in a science fiction movie, and she cannot quite wrap her mind around it, but it is happening for her so she cannot deny it. What has occurred is that her brainwaves are altered because of the breathing and guided meditations added to her now acute observations. She is usually too busy talking about her life in her head, and her brain is usually blipping along at a rapid rate. Melanie is also feeling something else she has rarely felt in her life; a sense of peace and contentment outdoors.

This peace of mind can occur due to a culmination of twenty-four hours of consciousness expanding activities. She has stated an intention at least three times. She has experienced three guided meditations, and a Cellular Theta Breath Meditation. She has been observing her mind and writing about her creation of reality along the way, all accompanied by thought and emotion provoking music. Right here on this threshold of observing the outside world, nature, the universe, she is viewing reality from her new expanded consciousness for the first time in her life. She has awakened.

Janna, on the other hand, has been awake off and on for some time now. She is also viewing her surroundings much like Melanie, only without the surprise, but with deep gratitude. Janna is also observing an expanded world around her, and she has been seeing the world more this way ever since she attended the retreat last time. Oh yes, she falls back into her normal routines and forgets this way of viewing reality for a while, but she will eventually remember it again. It is that remembrance that made her want to come back to this retreat, be fully in this experience again, and to bring her best friend. 'I just wish everyone could see and feel the way I do right now. The world would be a better place if everyone could just wake up.'

Deanna is having a hard time right now. It is very quiet and her mind is talking negatively as they walk. She feels jealous of the friendship that Janna and Melanie have with each other, even though they are not excluding her. They seem to be sharing some kind of experience she cannot find. She is feeling very open and that feeling is a little scary, like maybe she could be in some kind of emotional danger. Deanna is a woman of chaos. She creates and lives in chaos to avoid silence, to avoid her inner self. Unfortunately though, if she doesn't take the journey to her inside, she will never fully experience the recovery she so desperately fights to keep every day of her life. One can only recover so far and so long before you must face yourself. The escape artist must find safety in being vulnerable, must feel that the universe is not out to get her, and in fact, will support her and lead her to a path that is much better than the one the mind would chose.

But right this minute, Deanna's mind is telling her to excuse herself for an afternoon nap to get away from these unpleasant feelings and thoughts. Deanna doesn't realize that her thoughts are creating the feelings that are creating more thoughts, which are in actuality blocking her experience of the world around her, the connection she so desperately craves, and in so doing, she pushes the potential for closeness out of existence. It is an illusion but a very real one for Deanna, right now.

'After all, the facilitators did say that we could go to our rooms after a short walk, and we could take a nap if we wanted or whatever we wanted to do. These girls won't miss me if I grab a few minutes of rest, would they?' She motions to Melanie and Janna with her hands next to her cheek, like she is sleeping and points toward the room. They look puzzled but nod as she trots off toward the room for some escape time. 'I need a cigarette.' Her mind is not content with only sleep for escape and now she seeks a drug as well. As she stops before crossing the dirt road, suddenly a deer bolts across the path about twelve feet away from where she now stands, frozen in fear. 'Wow, this must be one of those signs they were talking about. I didn't think deer would be around here this time of day.'

Factually speaking, we have rarely, if ever, seen a deer at this retreat site. The deer seems to have appeared for Deanna alone. The deer appears to be bolting away out of fear, escaping from Deanna, no threat at all to it, and in fact Deanna is quite the animal lover. The symbolic message doesn't escape Deanna, who realizes that she is much like the deer escaping in fear from two women who are quite willing at this point to love her. 'What is wrong with me?'

Nothing, would be the correct answer. She is just being overwhelmed by that survival system that is in place, the one that she has been developing ever since childhood. It takes a bit of practice before one can stand and face your fear. Or could that be more correctly stated as before you can stand and face your connection to love?

Chapter Eight Journal Questions

1. What does it feel like to you when you think about being connected to the universe as a whole living being?
2. Imagine that you are connected to something you like in nature, and can communicate with it, like a tree, bird, or flower. What do you hear it saying?
3. If you could hear rocks, trees, oceans, animals, all of creation, how do you think your life would be different?
4. If you could hear your own body talking, what do you think the parts would be saying?
5. What is your mind saying to you while you read this chapter?

Chapter 9 I Made It Up

"I have spent most of my time worrying about things that have never happened."
—Mark Twain (1835 - 1910)

"It ain't no use putting up your umbrella till it rains."
—Alice Caldwell Rice

"Please lie down and make yourself comfortable for a meditation." Once again, a facilitator is instructing the group to get ready for a guided meditation, but the room isn't relaxed. It is late afternoon and they have just returned back to the meeting room from their walks outside, spending some time supposedly together enjoying the environment, napping, or swimming. When they first returned to the room, the facilitators requested the group to participate in an exercise in which they are requested to accept a change without their permission. This activity has created an agitated energy in the air as music that appropriately matches the mood begins.

Before you read this meditation, can you think of a time long ago, maybe when you were in school, in which you were picked to be on a team or in a group of friends? Maybe you were the one who always got to choose teams or select the friends to be in your group, or maybe you were never picked and always felt left out? Perhaps you were always in the outcasts, or maybe you were popular? Or were you a follower? Can you remember how it felt to be in this type of position in your lifetime? Imagine also that you have been removed from one group and arbitrarily placed into another one with no warning, as if someone just came into your life and told you to change places. How would you feel?

Our participants have just experienced an activity that reminds many people of these times in your life when you did or didn't get chosen for a group, and how you would feel. This selection process seems to go on in life even today at work or elsewhere. It can take place in your mind when you sometimes think that perhaps others do or do not accept you into their circle. These participants are still thinking about how they feel in these positions when this meditation begins.

I MADE IT UP
(©Diane Donovan Vaughn, 1996)

"Stop... stop and think about how you feel right now.
  Are you happy?
  Are you sad?
  Are you mad or upset?
  Are you uptight or tense anywhere?
  Are you feeling disappointment?
  Are you feeling special?
  Are you in love with life?
  Are you happy with your life?
  Are you unhappy with it?
  How are you feeling?

"Think about how you feel about the last exercise. Think about the position you are in. Think about where you wanted to be, if anywhere. Are you in the position you want to be in? Do you like the position? Do you dislike the position? What does being in this position mean to you? Are you special to the rest of the people in the room because you are one of those picked to do

I Made It Up

the deciding? Or, does that position frighten you, and you think you are being put on the spot with little or no choice? Are you one of the people who are picked? What does that say about you? Is that good or bad for you? Are you one of the people who are not chosen? Does that mean that you are left out? Does that mean that you are not good enough in some way? Or do you breathe a sigh of relief at not having to be mixed with people you didn't know that well. Does it mean you aren't wanted? Does it mean you are not in the right group? Does it mean your buddies are bad? Do you think your buddies have something to do with the choices? If only you were in a different group, the results could be better... or worse. What if the larger group is now a group you have to work with? What if it means something very spiritual if you were picked or not picked? What if you have to... what if I have to... what if it means...?

"STOP! STOP YOUR MIND! STOP! Your mind fills with dozens of possible interpretations of the events. Your mind goes over every option until it comes up with the reality that it thinks is the most likely one. On what does it base its information? How does it come up with these apparent solutions for this situation? Your mind come up with these ideas like it does for all other situations. The mind made it up. The mind makes up your conclusions based on your past. The mind comes to conclusions based on your past.

"YOU MADE IT ALL UP. NOTHING HAPPENED HERE EXCEPT WHAT YOUR MIND MADE UP. Nothing happened. You made it up.

"Take several deep breaths and relax your mind and body. Imagine that you can see a white light surrounding you and filling you. Think about the last exercise and remember the feelings you experience during a choosing process. What are your feelings during that experience? Remember other times when you felt those feelings. What other times does this exercise

remind you of? What memory does it trigger? What is your pattern of relating to new situations? How do we continue living like this?

"You are in new situations all the time. Think about what happens.

"You see someone act in a certain way and you have a reaction. Your mind snaps into thought, into memory of past events. Quickly, the mind searches for meaning to the event. Just as quickly, the mind offers a survival solution, and causes the body to produce the appropriate chemicals.

"Now you have your reality defined... your reaction... an emotional reaction based on your past!

"You interpret their actions... the interpretation based on your thoughts, based on the past. You have your judgment of the others firmly in place, convincing you that you know what another person is doing. You judge! You judge others based on your past. And, if that isn't enough, you believe what you judge to be true, and an opinion is born...

"... an opinion that you will remember about them forever. From this time forward, you have an opinion about another that will change the way you see that person in the future. Now... your past... has become... your future! This process is how the mind operates to create us and them. This reaction, based on our past, is how we destroy our oneness. This is how we let the mind run our lives, abdicating our power, giving up to our past and letting our past create our future!

"Your past can create your entire opinion of someone.

> *STOP! Stop the mind.*
> *It doesn't have to be like this.*
> *It doesn't have to be like this.*
> *Remember love?*
> *Remember love.*
> *Remember the lesson!*

"Our only lesson is to love ourselves and allow this love to expand outward to encompass all that is.

"From your first emotional reaction, just remember love. Their actions are not about us. My actions are not about you.

"Your actions are not about them. It's all about the past, and survival. It's all being made up. Nothing happened. Nothing happened. Nothing happened. Your mind made it up.

"Your task is to stop believing that your reactions define the only true reality.

"Stop! Ask yourself, "Did I make it all up?"

"What part really happened and what part did my mind contribute? Does my mind know what is in the heart of the one I judge? What real threat exists here, and what part am I making up?"

"Do you know the difference? When will you know the difference? You will know when you stop believing the lie you make up out of your past? When you stop the mind and hear the heart. What harm can come to you if you love another? What harm if you love? Let the past be the past before it also becomes the future.

"Our only lesson is to love regardless of the actions of others. Stop! Does your mind rebel and start making up scenes or events in your past that you can never forgive? What do you think would happen if you just loved? Does the mind rebel and think about all the actions you would have to take which might leave you drained? Stop! Who said anything about actions? Love is a feeling, a state of being.

"Don't you feel the pain of the past flood through you when you think about how unforgivable or despicable someone's actions have been? Release your bond of hate or pain, and feel love flooding your heart like a warm golden liquid erasing the pain and soothing you. Why would you choose the path of hate and pain over love ever again? And why would you let pain rule *your heart when the sweet feeling of love can always be in your heart.*

"Always choose love.

"Everyone on this planet is simply trying to have more love in their lives.

"Sometimes they ask for it, and sometimes they cry for it. Don't judge the way that others are crying for it.

Just love them.

Just love them.

Let love be the solution for all things. Breathe.

"As long as you remember this lesson, as long as you remember to stop your mind and remember to love, your future will be one of endless love."

'Wow, I am shocked at how fast I lose my cool. One minute I felt so peaceful, and with this one exercise I was blown back into my whole negative reality. This is bad. How will I ever be able to maintain it when I get back home when I am so easily thrown off track?' Melanie is anxiously obsessing about the last exercise and meditation. For a moment, she thought she was losing something important. She felt like she lost control, a completely unacceptable concept for her mind. Quickly, she tried to find a way to regain control, and having failed, she was angry and upset.

The mind feels safe in the rut of sameness. By now, you have been noticing the themes of your mind, but have you really noticed what part of reality that the brain is adding to your experiences? It is like the fish in water. Does the fish really notice the water? Ninety-nine percent (I am making up that figure for the sake of simplicity, and who really knows) of what the brain tells you is happening with others is incorrect! Why am I making up the percentage? I am using it to demonstrate how inaccurate you could be when you think you can read the mind of another person. A psychic will tell you that when it comes to their own realities, they feel they could be very inaccurate! The issues you have, the thought forms you carry in your mind will determine and warp your view of reality.

Reality of belief is based on everything that has happened to you from the beginning of your life. As your mind categorizes life and constructs beliefs based on these events, your reality begins to be created around these thought forms. What are thought forms? They are like contextual fixed points in the brain that take on an almost sacred quality. They are points that define reality for you so that you don't question the world around you anymore. By the time you are five years old, you have placed many experiences into these categories, and may no longer experience the categories as new when you encounter them again, even dismissing them from your view entirely.

The really funny thing about the mind is in its ability to generalize, and to do it so inaccurately. Take the example that as a child, your mother was a severe alcoholic. Your mind learns from the major female role models in your life to build this category of women. In other words, your mind will say that all women behave like your mother, and in this case that all women are like an alcoholic mother. You have alcoholic beliefs to contend with even if you never touch alcohol. Your mother gives you the category in which you define all females as undependable and irrational, while at the same time maybe instilling you with the hope that one will not disappoint you. If you are a woman, you distrust yourself and women. If you are male, you distrust females. All the while, your mind may be waiting for women to disappoint you.

These beliefs are like the water around the fish. What does your mind make up from your past that you are not noticing?

The mind would be more accurate if it said that practicing alcoholic females are often undependable and irrational, rather than all women are. But the mind generalizes the belief about our mother to all females, sober or alcoholic. After all, you form this thought system when you are learning about your environment, at less than five years old.

You see in this way, the reality of belief is simply quite inaccurate. You can literally grow up to fear females because of your mother, or to fear males because of your father. Your mind is generalizing out to one-half of the planet because of the actions of one person!

Since you have been watching your mind throughout the book, you are aware of some of your beliefs. What happens when you become aware of some beliefs is that you stay unaware of others. Then, what happens when you get triggered is that you can immediately relapse into negative thinking, mind reading, and judgment. Remember, the mind has its survival system that focuses on problems as a crucial activity to ongoing survival. That system is good if you are in danger, but can be too reactive, too controlling and downright domineering of your reality.

What can you do when you get triggered into relapse if you are not in real danger? Suspend the thoughts that cause you pain for a moment, and expand your thought processes. Take deep relaxing breaths, chant, pray, and move your consciousness. What would you like to happen? When triggered, the mind is usually focused on a problem not on a solution. What is a solution? Where would be a good place to focus your power, your intentions? If you are focusing on your problems with all your mental, emotional, and verbal power, then you are going to continue to create these kinds of problems in your life. Where do you want to focus your power?

Start directing that powerful brain of yours onto an intention of being, rather than reacting! Return your focus to your peaceful intention? Redefine your meaning of the words: *focus* and *intentions*. One definition of *focus* is to concentrate attention or effort. (Webster's 9th) If you check the definition, you find that it speaks of rays of light. This connection of the word *focus* with rays of light would be a great way to visualize this process. *Intention* is defined as intensity, which in turn means the quality or state of being intense. (Webster's 9th) Focusing the intention could be said to be concentrating your attention or effort, directing the light intensely on your solutions. Look at the definitions together again. Concentrate attention or place forth effort intensely. It is like shining a light in the dark.

No discussion of intention would be complete without mentioning the difference between intention and affirmation, since affirmations are commonly used to manifest reality. Affirmation, by definition, is a positive assertion. In other words, I create a positive statement like, "I am rich" to positively affirm money into my life. Some may take exception to the words, "I am rich" preferring the words, "I have abundance". The preference is significant to some, but taking exception is focusing on the problem again! Many people teach the correct way to phrase affirmations. I recommend that you read Louise Hay and Florence Shinn to learn the art of positive language. It is within language and changing it that you can create new realities. Speech and the sounds from the voice box have the power to alter your reality. If you doubt this, then say something to another person that they don't want to hear and watch how your reality alters. If you are like most, you are minimizing the words that arise almost effortlessly, flowing out of your mouth. These words mimic the way you think. These words are the verbal representation of how you are creating your reality.

Watch your language. You may think you are speaking positively when you say something that starts with "I want..." Look at "I want" as "I lack" and you will see that your story is one of not being able to get what you want. If you have success, your story will change to "I have" or "I am" language.

After learning to speak a positive language, you can go deeper and deeper. Focusing your intention is a deep form of changing reality. When I say changing reality, I don't mean that one reality is wrong and another is right! Many realities exist simultaneously. Many people are most often caught in one that they would like to alter. Having a desire to alter your life usually occurs because you are not happy with what you are currently creating. How did you help create this reality?

For example, let's look at relationships that create pain. Imagine that you have a relationship that you find painful. But, let's also say that you have always had relationships that are painful, and now you realize that you seem to be a magnet for bad relationships. In these hypothetical circumstances, you cannot find a good relationship by simply escaping the current one and looking for another, because you have tried that in the past. If you buy a good affirmation book, you could begin phrasing affirmations that sound like this: "I have a wonderful, fulfilling relationship with the man/woman of my dreams." You repeat this statement to replace the negative words you customarily use to describe your relationship such as: "I have such a bad relationship." What will begin to happen is that you will draw more available single people to you when you persist in doing this activity. But, and this is a big but, you will also be drawing the belief you have about men/women to you. In other words, you have to alter your belief that good men/women don't exist, and other beliefs you have about relationships. A client of mine repeated her belief to me when she said, "I am not attracted to nice guys. They are boring." Do you see how those two statements restrict reality? She is making it up.

A persistence factor arises in all this talk about changing reality. Saying an affirmation one time will not usually work because you will not believe it right away. Obviously, if you believed it immediately, it would work faster. Focusing the intention involves persistence. This is why affirmations and focusing the intention work very well together. In other words, if you are going to make up reality, what reality would you like to create instead of the one you are currently doing?

Right now would be a good time to get out your journals and write an affirmation that you are willing to repeat every time you usually obsess on something negative. It would be OK to have two things in the affirmation such as: "I am rich and healthy." All that means is that you have those two beliefs linked together in some way. For example, "I can't be healthy unless I am rich." See how the mind likes to link things together? Make sure when you write your affirmation that you are using positive language. "I am healthy" is not the same statement to the brain as "I am not sick." The brain hears "I am sick" and forgets the "not".

When you are looking at your beliefs, look at how you may be linking beliefs in some type of a double bind. These mental statements sound like if you get your way, you will suffer in another way. "If I am married, I will be trapped." "If I have children, I will be a bad parent." "If I have a good relationship, it will be boring." Finding these linking double binds is imperative if you want to improve your motivation to succeed. For example, why would you want to meet a great person to have a relationship with if it would be boring? It is actually a common belief that the lack of chaos is boring! An affirmation to counteract that belief would sound something like, "I am now enjoying peace." With the relationship bind, you could say, "I am in a great relationship with a wonderful person, and we are excited to be with one another." The mind likes to limit reality simply because it has never viewed the alternative, in fact, it doesn't believe that it exists.

By the way, positive affirming communication is especially helpful with children. The emotional mind is like a three-year-old after all. Use the words you want, not the words you don't want. For example, "Be quiet" is not processed the same as "Stop talking". In the first case, the child hears the word, 'quiet'. In the second case, the child hears the word, 'talking'. The mind is like a child. It hears where you focus your energy.

Write your affirmation now. Keep it short. Also write the negative statement you are replacing. The next step, of course, is to catch your mind in the midst of that negative statement and replacing it with the positive. But for now, after you have the positive statement, repeat it 100 times. Do this repetition daily, or even more often. It can be a little chant you use to occupy your mind when your mind is determined to think negative thoughts. Remember, this could be as simple as changing "I need to lose weight," to "I am the perfect weight." "I need to go to the gym" to "I love going to the gym."

If your mind is talking to you about all the reasons that your affirmation cannot be true, then listen intently to the reasons. Listen and write those negative statements in your journal. These statements are keys to unlocking the solution.

Here is an example of how the mind talks about an affirmation. "I can't be in a good relationship because I am in a bad one. I can't get divorced because of the kids. I am afraid to be on my own. I have done this before and I always fail. What's the use? There are no good men/women out there." These are just a few examples of the endless ways in which the mind can talk about your perceptions of reality. For now, just repeat the affirmation instead of letting the mind drone on and on about its doubts. If you repeat the affirming phrase instead of letting the negative talk go on and on, you can stop a negative spiral of thinking, at the very least. Do not let your mind get caught up in how to create your goal. Focusing on a goal creates the how.

Keep returning again and again to the persistence of focus! You are focusing on something all the time! As a matter of fact, your intentions are constantly manifesting. You learn to focus your intentions in childhood. You are told where to focus your intentions. You are shown through imprinting with your parents about how to focus your intentions. They show you the subjects on which to focus. Your past determines your present, and your present determines your future through the focus of your intentions.

I want you to experience the focus of your intentions now. Go back to your affirmation. Where have you been focusing your intention in regard to your affirmation? Notice in the case of "I have a bad relationship." Where would I be focusing my intention with that statement? I am directing my attention, intensely on "bad relationship." If you read the book *Handbook to Higher Consciousness*, by Ken Keyes (1976), he will go on to tell you that if you are having an emotional reaction to your negative statement that you are in fact addicted to it. In other words, you would be addicted to the bad relationship in the example above.

Once you accept that you are addicted to your realities, you can begin to understand the magnitude of the undertaking to change your view. And you will return to the word focus or persistence again and again. It seems like work, but it is no more work than you are currently doing with your unsatisfying focus. A peaceful, loving focus is like the sun glistening across a smooth lake. A negative focus is like being sucked into a whirlpool of sludge.

Think about an alcoholic for a minute. Many of you may not be aware of the dynamics of alcoholism, but you will understand much more if you look at the problem from the level of focus. The alcoholic is focused on alcohol. The alcoholic is always thinking about when they are going to party, who will be at the party, where the party will be held, and of course, where are the best places to obtain the best deals on alcohol. Happy Hour is made for alcoholics. Not having the addiction to alcohol, Happy Hour annoys me. The waiter brings two drinks for the price of one, and I only want one. The people are extremely loud, and the energy is chaotic. I don't like or look for Happy Hour because luckily alcohol is not one of my intentions! I literally focus on being somewhere else during that time of day. Since I live in Las Vegas, Happy Hour is a big deal here. Drunk people gamble more freely; another addictive focus.

Do you get the picture of the difference in focus? Every addiction is defined by focus. Often times, an addict will say that they could stop if they want to. Being able to stop for a time is not the same as changing focus. Changing focus is defined by persistence. And persistence is not something that occurs for a week, a month, or a year. For example, being a non-smoker, having quit for many years, means that you are maintaining your focus continually. At any time, you could lose your focus easily if you have the addiction.

Affirmation experts sometimes take exception with alcoholics continuing to say in Alcoholics Anonymous meetings, "I am an alcoholic." This statement appears to be an affirmation creating drinking. Why it doesn't create drinking in some people is because of the focus of intentions. Where is the intention focused? If the intention is focused on realizing that the person has the addiction to alcohol and is focused on recovery, then the person is not creating drinking, but is creating recovery.

Sometimes, a so-called negative affirmation creates positive results. I use it myself on occasion and teach it in therapy. Some people say, "My money is terrible right now," and their money problem will get worse and worse. Other people will say the same statement and will make more and more money! The difference is in focusing intention. When the person creates less and less, they are focusing their intention on all the ways they have less and less. The person who makes more and more is focusing their intention on ways to make more and more. And watch the language of the two types of people. The one person will talk about where they can go to increase money, and the other person will talk in a more hopeless theme about how depleted they are and how scarce their sources of money are, even failing to acknowledge the money they do have.

With the negative affirmation, one might post a sign in the house that reads, "You are going to be broke the rest of your life." In this case, the mind would fight the statement in rebellion with a, "Hell no! I am not. I am going to make lots of money." See how the intention shifts.

Focusing your intention is a miracle. It is astounding in every way, when you realize that you can change your focus and change your reality! If we are making it up, making up reality, then chose to make up a reality you like, and make it one that benefits everyone in the world.

Where would you place your focus? Do you want to focus on peace, love, and compassion? If so, you are a healer. If you are holding a peaceful, loving, compassionate focus, then you are healing yourself, and the world right along with you. If you could hold this focus for an hour a day, the world would be improving for that hour.

Remember that when you are in a room full of people one negative person can affect the whole room. So too, can one peaceful, loving, compassionate person. Of course, holding the focus in the face of negativity is the challenge, isn't it? If you get past your own negativity, you also have to be able to hold it around the negativity you feel from others. It is easy to get distracted. Just keep refocusing.

When you are consciously focusing your intention, you are on the healing road. You are a healer of others no less. And the ways in which you heal yourself and others are as varied as the people themselves. But you may wonder why people cannot find healing sometimes? Why won't one technique work on everyone? It won't, you know. Healing occurs because of many factors. One technique will bring one person a miracle healing but leave another completely unchanged. The path of each person is found deep within, and no one, often not even the person themselves knows the truth.

There is only one person you can truly seek to know and that is you. And you can become adept in more than one form of healing. Then, you can take whatever forms of healing that you use, add it to Cellular Theta Breathing and become even more powerful. Focus your intention to heal. Healers are just as sidetracked by their mental thought forms as other people, maybe more so. Refocusing your mind to healing and off of survival is the path that makes you a powerful healer.

When you practice many forms of healing, you begin to notice a connection to the source of all healing. Take a form like Reiki. Reiki is an extremely powerful form of energy healing. In Reiki, you are initiated by someone who has been initiated in a system that has been passed along from one generation to another. You can trace a lineage when you are initiated. Energy flows from your hands and into the person on whom you are working. It is powerful. On some, you will create a temporary relief in their condition, and on others, a complete healing.

Massage along with Healing Touch is enhanced when you are initiated into Reiki. Do you see how each technique can add to the next? Combine the breath, enter Theta and slow down your brainwave. The energy you are feeling will literally talk to you.

Healing by another is always possible if the healer is well trained, right?

Wrong! When you have a session with me, I am trained in Reiki, Rebirthing, Cellular Theta Breathing, Pranic Healing, and many forms of psychotherapy along with hypnosis. Even with all these powerful healing modalities, the healing depends on the patient. I may be very adept at enlisting your cooperation because I am a therapist, but I have to enlist both your conscious and unconscious cooperation. As a matter of fact, you may be totally unaware of the real problem. Fritz Perls, (Perls, Hefferline, Goodman, 1979) the coauthor of Gestalt therapy said that clients do not come to therapy to get healed; they come to get a better neurosis. In other words, the client wants to keep doing what they are doing and get different results. Yes! I want to keep eating everything I eat right now, and lose weight. It has not worked that way yet, by the way.

The very best healer cannot change your free will. The best healer helps you to help yourself. Do not lay any guilt at your feet because of any illness you have. Many who hear they can create reality then start judging everyone around them about their negative creations, or possibly, you might start judging yourself. Remember, that is how your mind starts making it all up, and judging is not solution oriented.

Guilt is not healing except as an indicator that you desire to change something that gives you discomfort. Guilt signifies that you are aware of the wrongness of how a situation feels for you.

Words alone do not create your illness. Illness and pain are often ways in which our body is speaking to us. However, words with intention can create, and can help you find a cure for what ails your life! Begin by asking your body what it wants you to know, to do, to hear. When you listen to your body, then you will more fully know how to formulate your intentions. Cooperation is the key word here.

Remember that repeating words combined with intention, known as focus, creates more powerfully than ever. Are you focusing on being healed, on a world of abundance and peace?

It does no good to say with intention, "I can't get well," or "I can't... (add any word)" because obviously, "I can't" eliminates possibility. You are making it up again.

Let's say you go to the doctor for a rash. The doctor gives you a shot and the rash leaves. Then, you have a stomach pain for months. He prescribes medications that control your symptoms, never telling you that the shot caused your stomach problems. This example really occurred to me. I was taking stronger and stronger medicines for my stomach. I could easily say, "I tried everything I was supposed to try and I can't get any better." Do you think I would keep looking for something else when the doctor says I have tried everything there is to try? Of course, the doctor is lying but he doesn't really know that he is lying. He is telling the truth on his level. Truthfully, he has given me everything he will give me, but that is only a small fraction of what is possible.

I bought a book written by another doctor (Hoffman, 1990) and cured that bout with my stomach problems by drinking aloe vera juice. I threw away my medicine and cured my problem. I didn't cure the cause of my ongoing stomach problems but I cured the cause of that outbreak. The steroids they gave me for my rash bothered my already sensitive stomach. Doctors quite often prescribe steroids for many conditions. Many other alternatives, holistic approaches are superior to steroids. But these approaches are not often found at the doctor's office. Go to the doctor, but don't think that the doctor is all that exists for healing. Remember to ask yourself about your conditions, and remember to listen.

Take responsibility for your healing. The best healer is helping you fight your contribution to the creation of illness, which may be your need to hear something important about your life that your body is shouting with illness. In trying to heal yourself, you are altering your creation of illness. What is the cause of my stomach being the first organ to be affected with illness? Other people would not get the stomach pain from the shot. I got the rash. I got the stomach pain. These illnesses are my unique energy system reactions to my life. The stomach is talking. The body is talking. Pain is the body communicating with you. Listen to it.

Remember that the first line of defense with illness is to communicate with the illness. Say to your rash, sore throat, stomach, "What do you want from me?" Quiet the mind and listen in silence. Meditate by watching (observe) the mind, when you ask the question, "What do you want from me?" Listen to the response in your mind to the question.

Amazingly, small problems, like the beginning of a sore throat will respond so well to communication (could it be because the throat is the center for communication) that speaking to the pain and answering the pain could relieve it totally.

Say to your sore throat, "What do you want from me?" The throat says, "I want you to stop talking on the phone with so and so."

Now the answer that you would give to your throat's request to stop your long phone chats is quite important. It is a good idea to agree if you want your throat to stop hurting! And you have to mean it. If you say to your throat that you will stop talking on the phone to so and so, then your sore throat will stop hurting. Yes, it will stop hurting until you break your promise to your throat.

If you are one of those people trying this experiment right now, who says that their body will not answer, then meditate on the question every spare minute for the next twenty-four hours. Hopefully, the answer will come to in the way of a dream, or, and this is funny, by way of a messenger. Someone you meet will tell you the answer. Make sure that you are listening inside and outside for the answer, because the answer is coming.

If you are one of those people trying this experiment right now who are getting an answer you do not like such as, "Quit fighting with your husband, daughter, son, etc," then meditate on how to accomplish the advice you hear; in this case, how to quit fighting. One thing is certain and that is if your body is in pain or sick in some way, then it is trying to communicate with you. Listen to it.

Remember that everyone is always trying to solve problems with solutions that don't work! In the example of fighting, you can rest assured that if you don't know how to fight, then fighting doesn't work. You may think that you are trying to communicate but it ends up being a fight. You may have the best intentions (Remember hell is paved with good intentions) but your intentions are mixed up, and are not the best intentions if they cause a fight. Look at your result and then you will know about your confused intentions. If your result is not what you wish to create, then your intention is not what you think it is. The mind has the capacity to mislead you so thoroughly that you will continue doing the same nonproductive communication over and over and still expect a different result. The mind is a liar.

For example, your intention may be to improve your husband's health by talking to him about his bad habits. Examine your intention along with your motive. Why are you focused on him to begin with? Is your answer, "Because I love him"? Go deeper because you were focused on fear and "I love him" is not the only reason you brought up the subject of his health. You brought up the subject of his health because you are afraid also. The communication of your good intention ("I love him") may be inaccurately conveyed because your unconscious intention is "I am afraid." Your husband could respond to your fear with resistance, and suddenly you have the fight. Fear communications often result in fighting. You have to be a completely serene, peaceful, highly evolved individual to not respond to fear with fear.

Fear creates fear. Love creates love. By the way, some

people are very reactive to any fear you may project, and overreact very strongly. Just notice when you have these kinds of communications that the other person is not receiving your loving intention at all, and only perceives fear from you.

When your body has illness, you can have fear. The task is to find the fear and release it. Yes, it can be a journey, which may be its purpose to put us on the journey of observing ourselves, and becoming more than our minds. Maybe we are here to disbelieve fear? But whether that statement is true or not, releasing fear often relieves pain and illness, and can improve all your communications.

As a therapist and facilitator, I am working on releasing my own pain. I am writing to inspire you to release your fear and find your bliss in life. Am I without pain? No. However, I do experience bliss quite often.

What is bliss anyway? Well, it is something you get from personal growth, from being a healer, and from creating a reality of bliss.

Who is the healer? You heal yourself and as you heal yourself, you heal each other. I hear people say all the time that they are tired of all this personal growth. I agree. So am I. But what are you here for? Are you here to flip TV stations? Are you here to go from one addiction to another? Are you here to have one cigarette after another? People tell me that their addictions give them pleasure. I agree. I have smoked two packs a day in my past. I know that when I smoke a cigarette, I feel good at the moment. Then, the next moment, I want another and another, until I am a slave every fifteen minutes the rest of my life to that next one. What kind of life is that? It is not blissful.

Today, I am committed to personal growth. Why? I am addicted to bliss. I love to be in bliss. I never had bliss with cigarettes. I never had bliss from TV. I never saw a cocaine addict continue to have bliss for more than a moment before the crash. What if you could stay in bliss for longer and longer periods of time? What if bliss was simple and free?

Bliss from within is found in other dimensions, and within the petal of a flower. How we reach bliss is simply to be. And simply being is quite difficult for us when we are using addictions, seeking thrills, doing, doing, and doing. It's not that we can get by in life by doing nothing, but doing is not all there is. Bliss happens when you stop listening to the fantasies of the mind and become completely present.

Bliss arrives from within and graces us with compassion and love. It allows us to be entertained by the moment. Why do you think the guy sits with his legs crossed meditating? It lowers his blood pressure and takes him to a state of bliss. Cellular Theta Breathing can help guide you to enlightenment, and is one of the fastest ways that I have discovered to this point. And yet the mind will fight doing Cellular Theta Breathing because the mind seeks thrills and survival. The mind can love that a drug like nicotine makes you relax and have energy at the same time. The mind can think that nicotine is a great solution. This mistake is another example of the limitation of the mind, of the mind making it up.

The brain seeks instant gratification, even though in the long run something like cigarette smoking is a huge threat to our survival. Different minds have different addictions. Scientists say the addictions we have may be in the genetic makeup or our cells. We inherit them from our ancestors. But what we do with our genetic makeup can be overridden by our higher self. What you hear at an Alcoholics Anonymous meeting is that a power higher than yourself can help you regain your sanity. Why do you need a higher power for that task? If you have been listening to your brain for a while, you may have now noticed how much it tends to lie and exaggerate. Perhaps it is not to be trusted with helping you make the correct choices?

You do not find bliss or your higher self in your mental belief structure. You find bliss and the higher self in stillness, in meditation, in hypnosis, in the breath. Really, all you have to do is shift your focus from the outside to the inside. Personal growth is about going from the outside to the inside. I have heard people say that personal growth is an addiction. Yes, it can be. It can be used as avoidance as well. I have seen people including myself avoid responsibilities using personal growth. Remember, within anything one can be swooned, carried away from your daily responsibilities. It all boils down to integrity really. Keep your commitments, and do not make excuses. Take responsibility for your life and its creation. Create your bliss, a bliss that is the highest good for the world.

Cellular Theta Breathing is a tool, not the destination. Yoga is a tool, not the destination! But then again, if you are carried away from taking care of business, perhaps you are being fooled again by the mind. Keep observing. Observe your thoughts, feelings, emotions. Observe your goals and observe the results in your life. If you don't feel good, if your goals and results are not good, then the secret will be found in your focus, your intentions.

You are having a human experience. A whole person is grounded on the planet, and full of love and compassion. You are still doing an Earth life and you are happy. How many happy people do you know? I mean the kind of happy; glowing from the inside out happy people do you know today?

Do happy people become unhappy people when disaster hits? No. They get sad but they have a bigger picture. When you are living in the present, in a blissful nature, then you have an abiding peace during disaster. Bliss is more than just happiness. Bliss is an experience of the universe as one huge expansion with no beginning and no end. Within the context of the so-called disaster, the blissful person sees that disaster as an illusion, at the same time comprehending and feeling the pain that exits within the disaster.

Unhappiness results when the mind convinces you that sadness, disappointment, limitation is all there is. Basically, the made up story is when your mind limits your reality, gets so involved in explaining reality, limiting reality, judging reality that you forget to notice the ever-expanding now in which you exist. This present is the one in which you are the captain of your ship sailing in a sea of endless energy, the energy of love and compassion. When you stop the mind making it all up and just be for a second, you will experience healing. You will be a healer to the world around you and you will know bliss.

Right now, our participants are having their own experiences with making up realities, with happiness and sadness. They finished with their made up stories, journal questions, then trotted off in silence to dinner and have now made their way to a circle outside, along with their sleeping bags. They are preparing to practice Cellular Theta Breathing under the stars. We don't always have this activity at Destiny. It really depends on the location, the time of year, and the weather, of course. But today everything is cooperating.

Janna is lying on her pad and sleeping bag, gazing at the moonless sky. It is clear and dark, with stars glistening in a panoramic show. 'You never see stars like this in town. Even if I look, it is like the stars cannot shine with all the light around town. I so look forward to seeing them again when I come here. It looks like a spiral in the sky above my head, and I have never seen anything quite like it.'

Madison is excited. She has never seen this many stars in her life. It feels a little scary being outside, and she is worrying a little bit about bugs, and feeling almost like that huge sky could swallow her whole. In fact, Madison grew up in the big city with few stars visible compared to this vista. She is wishing she could text her friends on her cell phone. 'Oh, it is so hard to be without my phone. I miss my friends. Honestly, what could it hurt to text for a few minutes?'

Madison's mother, Sophia, feels rather neglected by her daughter. 'She never does the buddy activities with me like everyone else. It is like being alone to be here with a teenager. She's probably not having a good time.' It seems that Madison got her beliefs right out of her mother's head, as now her mother has the same thoughts Madison has been having about her all day.

Ah! How soon we forget the lessons we just went through. The last exercise, "I Made It Up," refers to how the mind creates reality from sensory input, and how we totally believe our fantasy. Here, Sophia has decided how Madison feels without even asking her, since she has been respecting the silence with her daughter and cannot ask. Madison is actually enjoying herself, except that her mother annoys her, which is somewhat typical of teenage girls. In learning independence, teenagers sometimes use irritation as a way of asserting that independence. Her mother mistakenly assumes that energy must mean that Madison is displeased with the whole experience. Just hours from the insight of now, the mind lies and makes Sophia feel the fool about her own daughter.

Softly, they are settling into their sleeping bags on the red dusty ground, surrounded with mysterious rustling sounds of nature. Short trees and sage combine with the high desert dryness to create a unique odor when inhaled for this breath session. Music is beginning, with sacred chanting voices and haunting melodies, music to lull one into theta dreams. Ancient words in the music and the hypnotic sounds combine with foreign spirituality, creating an air of expectation. In fact, the vocal performers are people engaging in spiritual practices from various cultures in forms of worship, against a seductive background of music. Most of the words are from native languages and cultures.

The facilitator is adding some expressions to her usual 'prayer' before the breath. "I open a spiral in the sky and ask for the presence of luminous beings. May everything that comes forth, come forth from the light, and everything that is released, be released into the light." She also reminds people to ask for protection from God or their higher power. Earlier on in the evening, they had a ceremony with drumming, and experienced an altered state of consciousness induced by the drums. Now, chanting and intentions for luminous guidance are added to the breath session.

As Janna gazes into the sky, she is focusing on a spiral in the star pattern, and wonders again if it has always been there. 'Did I see that the last time I was here?'

Moments later, an Indian with a haunting flute background chants a prayer. As he finishes, a coyote howls in the music. Surprisingly, the coyotes begin to howl in the high desert surrounding this circle of breathers. Even the facilitators haven't had this experience before. These coyotes are a welcome sign tonight as everyone drifts into theta.

Stargazing with Luminous Beings

The facilitator doesn't explain the meaning of her comment about luminous beings and spirals in the sky to the participants, as it is a mystical suggestion that the participants become aware of the spiraling galaxy of which we humans all belong. The luminous beings are the luminous fibers of light that can be seen in the sky in the starlight, or in the light of the human beings on the ground breathing. In fact, from a certain space, humans would truly be rotating galaxies of light as well. These are the luminous beings.

Being outside like this, breathing, finding the theta state, connecting to the Earth as you lay on the ground, gazing into the starlight, listening to sacred chanting from around the globe, a spiritual experience unfolds for many. That experience may be to discover your luminosity along with your mysterious connections with the rest of the universe. Within that experience, you might feel a relationship to an angelic presence within, which you will be meeting tomorrow after your next breath session.

This luminous expanded state of consciousness is one of viewing the world from the point of view of the spiritual conception of your life. When you listen to this luminous connection, you hear more of the meaning of life whispering, calling you to your destiny, which is why we are here tonight so that you may have this experience.

As you read these pages, perhaps you would like to make a plan to visit a place in nature where the stars still shine brightly as they do especially with a new moon. It is best to do this activity when the moon is absent from the sky, since the stars will be the brightest. Get away from the lights of town and lie down on the ground. Bring your music along. Play some beautiful music like *Mystic Traveler* (Spheeris) as you take deep connected breaths. Look into the sky and take slow deep breaths. You can practice any breath techniques that you like to use. You can use the one in which you are observing the pauses in your breath pattern. You can use the one in which you count to six as you inhale, count to three holding your breath, and count to six as you exhale called six-three-six. You could use a repetitive drumming to induce an altered state of consciousness.

Take someone with you if you feel more comfortable, someone to observe the stars and sky in all its magnificence with you, in silence. For some, this is a childhood experience. For some, gazing into the night sky has never been experienced because the night sky has always been the sky of the city. As you focus on your breath, the music and the sky, move your consciousness to the stars. The starlight is traveling across the universe, the light flowing into your eyes and into your body. Become one with the starlight energy.

Gaze into the stars, the Milky Way and look into the spiral in the sky. Ask for the luminous beings connected to your own luminous being to whisper to you about your destiny in life. Remember to listen. Now you are practicing being one with the luminous beings. Imagine that the luminosity is the same luminosity that creates the light within you, and the light in the sky. Light and sound fill you as you gaze into the stars. Continue looking and being one with the starlight until the music finishes. May you find your own luminous connection and your destiny with this activity.

When the participants finish their breath session, a fire is lit. They are invited to look into the fire, warm themselves, and then slowly walk back to their room while they ponder the thought of being one with the starlight, the luminous being, the coyote, the fire, each other, and the universe. As usual, they attempt to practice silence and continue to journal their mind talk.

Chapter 9 Journal Questions

1. What does your mind make up?
2. What kind of energy do you sense about others that creates discomfort in you?
3. How does your mind create and lose focus?
4. What does your mind think about being healed, and about being a healer?
5. How do you feel about the thought of being a luminous being?
6. What happened for you when you watched the starlight and

considered yourself a part of a star?
7. What would you hear from your luminous connection to the rest of the universe?

Chapter 10 Integrating Love & Fear

"It's just a ride and we can change it any time we want. It's only a choice. No effort, no work, no job, no savings and money, a choice, right now, between fear and love. The eyes of fear want you to put bigger locks on your door, buy guns, close yourself off. The eyes of love instead see all of us as one."
–Bill Hicks

"Real, constructive mental power lies in the creative thought that shapes your destiny, and your hour-by-hour mental conduct produces power for change in your life. Develop a train of thought on which to ride. The nobility of your life as well as your happiness depends upon the direction in which that train of thought is going."
–Laurence J. Peter (1919 - 1988)

Saturday
Prayer Breathing

On the morning of the third day, the participants eat a subdued, seemingly thoughtful breakfast after a session of yoga and energy exercise. Once they enter the meeting room, they begin shuffling with their bedding, like puppies scratching for a comfortable position. Finally, they stop their moving and a somber facilitator begins the morning with an opening prayer (Williamson, 1994) about intimacy, setting the stage for a day of exploration of one's connection to self and to others, or the lack thereof. All of the facilitators posted around of the room are dressed in black, possibly for some reason known only to them.

Following a Cellular Theta Breath session, the group is now ready to experience a powerful meditation. This meditation will begin slowly, growing with intensity, and then relaxing into a journey of multidimensional realities. The participants seem to be sensing the importance of the journey they are about to take. They are making some noises, sneaking a snack and stalling a bit, even though they were asked to take a quick, silent bathroom and water break between the breath session and the meditation. As the music begins, the room's energy feels thick, like swimming in molasses. Melanie is wondering if the facilitators planned to dress in black or if it was an accident. She is still in a dreamy theta state from the prior breath session, and yet she feels vaguely unsettled and ill.

Integrating Love and Fear
(©Diane Donovan Vaughn, 1996)

"Close your eyes. Breathe deeply. Feel the life force entering your body, comforting you and soothing you. The breath is life. As long as you have your next breath, you have no problems. Pause for a moment and take an inventory of your life as it is, in the present.

"Relax into your surroundings and notice how peaceful your life is when you pay attention to the present. Imagine a pillar of white light and love around you. Notice any areas of tension in your body. Send the white light into those areas. Become one with those areas of tension, and ask them to speak to you about the problems that you have hidden inside your body.

"Ask your body, "What do you want from me?"

"Answer your body with a solution. The body is like a child; direct and in need. Comfort the body as you would a precious

child, with love and nurturing.

"Thank the body for sharing.

"Next, become one with the mind. The mind has the wonderful task of categorizing everything your senses bring to it. The mind has been alone in the task too long, being responsible for everything that occurs for you.

"Ask the mind, "What do you want from me?"

"Answer the mind with a loving solution. Sometimes, the mind will not believe the loving solution because for many years it has been solving your problems with fear. Encourage your mind to make a new commitment to choose love instead of fear. Now, thank the mind for sharing. Always thank your mind and body for sharing their information with you. Your mind and your body are gathering information and offering solutions to the best of their capacity, attempting to keep you alive, and instantly informed and gratified. Their only limitation is fear.

"Imagine for a moment that you are a very small child. Your view of life is one of a person who is about three feet tall. You see a different world around you than you do as an adult. As you see the world from this point of view, you begin to realize that you also hear things differently. You do not understand many things you hear or see.

"Now imagine that you are being put to bed. You are sleepy, but you fight going to bed. You fight, because you can. You fight, because you don't want to feel separation from the others. You fight, because you are afraid. But you go because you are a child and adults are making your choices for you. As you drift off to sleep, you drift into a deep and restless sleep. You begin to dream a nightmare. Perhaps you've had the nightmare before. You don't know the nightmare is a dream. You think the nightmare is real. You are the nightmare. Your breath becomes quicker and your heart beats faster. You are in fear and you bolt from your sleep crying for your parents.

Integrating Love & Fear

"How do you want someone to respond to you? Imagine that a loving adult comes to your side and hugs you, all the time whispering sweet comforting words: "It's OK. Everything is OK."

"They turn on a light so that you can see. "I will stay here with you as long as you need me. Everything is fine."

"They encourage you to look around and see that you are safe. "You are safe. I am here to protect you. I will keep you safe. I love you."

"As they speak their comforting words to you, feel your body begin to relax. Your breathing slows and the tension evaporates. How quickly the words of love and safety calm you.

"Take a deep breath. Relax and let the white light flow through your body like a river of white light washing away your tension and attachments to fear.

"Imagine that you are walking in a beautiful natural garden. See the beautiful shades of green all around you. All the colors of the rainbow are growing here, mingling with a multitude of shades of green. You are on a pathway that meanders through this medley of color. Smell the fragrance of floral scents combining with misty wetness in the air. The moist air caresses your nose as you breathe.

"Birds and small animals live in this garden, softly singing, chirping, and their skittering noises combine with the sound of your feet as you slowly walk and absorb this beauty.

"Here, you feel totally safe and serene. This garden is more beautiful than you have ever seen in your life, because you feel more safe and relaxed than you have ever been in your life. You are experiencing peace. You are able to see more clearly than you have ever seen. You are able to hear more clearly than you have ever heard. Touch something in your surroundings and feel the energy available to your touch. Everything is alive with energy. You are able to see the energy as well as feel it.

Surround yourself with light, and feel the power you have to use the light to relax and be inspired. Use the light to create beauty. Use the light to create safety. Use the light to create.

"*Walking along the path, the path widens and forms a circle around a sitting area with a lovely wooden bench. Overhanging the bench is a graceful willow branch from an immense tree. Surrounding the bench are many fragrant flowers. Squirrels live in the trees in this garden, and they are wondering if you brought any food for them. Create some nuts for the squirrels and feed them. Across from you, you see a large pond. This sitting area is for viewing the pond, which has beautiful white swans gliding among water lilies. As you melt into your surroundings, feeling the energy of being one with nature, you sense a presence beside you on the bench. The bench is large enough for three people and you are sitting in the middle of the bench. This presence that you are sensing beside you on the bench has now clearly become your inner child. This child represents all inner children you may have. The inner child part of you is that part that you may have forgotten; because you think that childhood no longer exists. When the child appears, you understand that you have this important part of yourself who still exists in childhood. Inside you, you have all the ages you have ever been before. They may not know about being an adult. They may not know about the present. They only know the past.*

"*Notice how the child looks. Notice how you feel toward the child. Sometimes, you may feel nothing. Sometimes, you may feel fear. Sometimes, you may feel disgust. Sometimes, you may feel love. Do not judge your reaction to the child, and do not judge the child. Instead, use the white light to keep you feeling safe and helping you to choose love. If you see the child, describe them. Make up a description if you don't see one.*

"*If you are content with how the child looks, bring the child very close to you on the bench. If you do not like the way the child looks, keep the white light protecting you and send light to the child. Use the white light and the beauty of the energy of the garden to renew and refresh your child. Let the true vision of the inner child unfold as the light spirals around the child and you. Now, view the real appearance of the child, who is perfect, whole, complete, and beautiful. Show the child your surroundings and enjoy them together.*

"Now, you begin to sense another presence next to you. You are still sitting in the middle of the bench with the child on one side of you. This new presence is your higher self. This higher self part of you is the perfect part of you. It is the part that knows about everything connected to the spiritual dimensions of the universe. This part may appear as an angel to you. Know that this part is really your angelic self. By finding this part of you, you are tapping into your own inner wisdom, which is the part connected to all others. Remember the incident with the nightmare. When a loving parent appears, it is as if an angel has appeared. This angel is you. This part of you is your future self, who knows all the answers. This part has already solved all the mysteries you have not solved. This one has evolved.

"Use the white light again to surround and protect you. If for any reason you feel fear, use the light to bring you back to love. Let the white light spiral around the three of you.

"The higher self has much wisdom to impart to you. What do you wish to know from your higher self?

"Ask the question and listen for the loving response.

"Ask the higher self about the inner child.

"What do you wish to know from your inner child?

"Ask the inner child, "What do you want from me?" Listen to the child.

"Ask your higher self, "What is a loving answer for the child?" Listen to your higher self.

"The higher self has the perfect parenting answers for you

anytime you need help. The higher self is your resource when dealing with your inner child.

"Answer the child with a loving answer.

Now, you are ready to become integrated with these two dimensions of yourself. You are a multidimensional being and this is your opportunity to become one with both your higher self and your inner child.

"Ask the inner child if the two of you could become one, and listen to the child's answer.

"If the child is reluctant or if you are reluctant, ask the child, "What will it take for you to be willing?" If you feel confused or do not understand how to help the child or yourself, ask the higher self for assistance to prepare you to be one with the child, and to prepare the child to be one with you. This agreement may involve a compromise between the two of you. You may have to agree to listen to the child and comfort the child. When the two of you are ready, take the child into your arms and allow yourself to become one with the child.

"Say, "I love you," to the child.

"Now, tell the higher self that you wish to become one with the higher self. Listen to the response of your higher self.

"Ask the higher self to allow a merging with you, and know that you and your higher self have always been one, but that you have not acknowledged your own perfection. Take a moment to feel the oneness of yourself and notice how complete and powerful you feel when you are whole.

"Hear the higher self say, "I love you."

"Feel the inner child's sense of wonder and discovery as your sense of wonder and discovery. Feel the higher self's sense of peace, compassion, and love as your peace, compassion, and love. See how these qualities complement your experience of your surroundings. Look around at the garden, the pond, and the animals, and notice how different, how expanded the energy has

become. Feel the light flowing through you again, and feel refreshed and new as you are in the river of white light. Continue to feel one within the river of pure white light.

"Allow yourself to stay in this new feeling of connectedness and bliss for a few moments. Any time you need wisdom, see the golden white light and access the perfected higher self part of you for your answers. With every experience, you can access that part of you that is childlike, wondrous, and in awe, as well as that part of you that is loving, compassionate, and peaceful. Together, you realize your multidimensional existence and create your life anew; a life of choosing your destiny of love."

What do you want from your life? What do you want from your mind and body? How did it happen that humans became disconnected from their own inner child, and from the inner wisdom that is readily available if only you would become silent and listen? How did we lose our connection to our home? Let's look at your relationship with fear and love to find your answers these questions.

Life is change. Buddha says that suffering is inevitable. Suffering arises in direct proportion to how attached a person is to maintaining a life the way it is in one moment of time, in your belief that something is going to stay the same and be totally controllable. Your attachment to a reality that the mind refuses to notice is always in flux can create fear, along with its companions of anxiety, anger, and depression. Fear without love leaves you devoid of meaning, absent of life satisfaction.

As a child, when left to your own devices, you may create many defenses as a way of dealing with change and distress that you encounter. It doesn't have to be an abusive reality to create defenses in a child. Often in adulthood, you will be surprised at how little it took to develop some serious life-altering reactions in a child's defense structure that will be carried along into adulthood, and accessed when you encounter the problems of everyday life. Defenses can be constantly engaged and love has become something else to be feared.

Integrating love and fear is experienced in a meditation at Destiny to help you incorporate a new way of looking at your past, your defenses, and to find that many defenses no longer serve the life of the person possessing it. Your defenses may actually be creating the results in your life that you do not like. To integrate love with fear creates power and life satisfaction.

Your higher power can become your strength rather than some of the worn out fearful defenses from the point of view of a child. And yet the child remains an important element in your life, for the child holds your power, your innocence, and your imagination. Ignoring any part of yourself like your childlike self or your fear will drain your energy, and can sabotage you from manifesting the life you desire. All parts of you are still important, no matter how old and wise you have become. But like all children, a parent is required for direction, especially when fear has been making your decisions.

The problem with parenting is that many use the same old parenting tactics with their own inner child that they encountered in childhood. These tactics are often filled with the fearful anxiety you encountered from your own parents. Parenting is always lacking to a child's mind, because parents are human beings and humans will always fail to be perfect (Freud). Parents are often neurotically anxious about a child's well-being and even though well-intentioned, this energy gets incorporated into the psyche of the child. In fact, if the parent was extremely angry and critical, the child can feel totally unloved! It is at these moments in development that a child could link love with pain, a link that can be broken.

It also may be where a person can obtain the idea that endless seeking for satisfaction, domination, or approval could be the best goals in life. Why, you may say, could that be true if you had good parents? Even good parents were never perfect in satisfying every need of a child, which may explain why all children develop defenses to deal with the surrounding reality. Remember also that humans have a genetic pattern that can create some powerful reactions due to personal brain chemistry. This pattern is influenced by the messages you receive growing up. Since this pattern is passed down to you by your ancestors, you cannot learn the most effective ways of dealing with your reactions from people reacting the same way, unless they have learned how to manage their own patterns first. Now, you have a chance to redirect yourself in a way in which you can choose the loving solution at last, and create peace with your fearful defenses.

Let's take a long look at fear and some of the many defenses that people employ. Change is often defined as a problem, which triggers fearful defenses like worry, anxiety, anger, and depression. These fears are a way of life for most of us. Worry is a killer with its slow lingering deteriorating condition of the body, also known as stress! Stress is tough on the body and mind, lowering your immune system and making you more susceptible to all forms of infections and illness. Look at the elderly and how stress like the death of a spouse can be a fatal experience to the survivor.

Stress comes in many disguises, often dressed as helpful! If change is occurring, notice your stress. Do you worry? Worry is about fear and survival thinking. What are your worries? If you are not worried, what else are you doing with the tension of your daily life? You may not be noticing stress because you don't think about it. You may think that you are handling it. Do you have pain or tension in your shoulders, back, neck? Stress manifests in the body as pain. The body is talking to you. Stress is occurring whether you observe it or not. If you don't notice what is stressing you out, then now is the time to start. Explore the mental processes of stress, which is a relationship with fear along with the many triggers of the mind. You will begin to see how to redirect your mental computer in the direction of peace in a maze of sensory stimuli, which your mind must categorize or ignore. Peace of mind includes peace of body, emotions, and feelings. Whether you notice it or not, you are often triggered into adrenaline responses that create stress every day, sometimes, every minute. Stress is based on fear.

Imagine that you are now solving your number one problem. How does it feel to be free of it? What would you have to do to solve it? If you don't have any idea how to get rid of the problem, or if all your attempts have failed, then ask an expert. For example, if the worry is about something like money, you could talk to a financial expert. If the worry is about something like death or sickness, you could talk to a doctor. However, talk as you may, your problems begin in your own mind, in your own past, and in your own processes of creation. The problem is about fear, and its lack of a connection to love. What do you fear? Have you heard that fear is an illusion? How could the fear you feel be an illusion? When you state that you have a problem, it would be a very good idea to notice the reality of the present moment. Is your problem present right now, or is it just present in your mind? Look at where you are sitting; the room, the space, the comfort and notice again. Are you in fact really suffering, or is your mind just torturing you?

If you don't know where to begin, and feel like you can't get anywhere with your problems, then you could see a therapist. A good therapist can help you identify your triggers as well as help you discover their origins. In therapy, you can derive the purpose you have for the way you think, and begin to unravel that purpose. You can create a new purpose for your mind, and decrease the mind's need to obsess or distract. You can find new ways to cope with problems, and even obtain information about the way your brain functions. For example, you could be obsessing but think that obsessing is normal, since you have always obsessed. You wouldn't know the difference if you have always been this way. Obsessing about problems is a waste of time, and often involves the mind in something that isn't currently occurring. For example, if you are thinking about being broke right now and about your bills, you might notice that you are not paying bills right now. Do you need money in this moment that you are reading this book? The mind often dwells on ideas that have no reality in the present. The mind entertains itself thinking about the past and the future, ignoring the present.

Imagine again that your number one problem is magically erased. Allow the relief to flood through you. You are free of that worry, but you will notice that worry number two quickly becomes worry number one. Look at your number two problem and you may begin to notice that problems seem to be never ending! Our minds are geared to find problems, fret over them, or wish that we could escape them.

A client will say to me, "Oh-h-h-h, I am so worried about money." If I tell a client that they can quit worrying and do relaxation, they often fight to keep their right to worry! "If I don't worry, I will never find a solution," they say. But when you are worrying, you are not problem solving, you are thinking about the problem, not the solution.

The big myth of the obsessive mind is that it perceives many more dangers than a mind that is not hyper vigilant. However, one cannot really say with any certainty that the one with the hyper vigilant mind is any safer! Saddled with a great high survivor brain, you are stuck in a world full of people that you are supposed to treat nicely. Being ready for any attack and prepared for any disaster will not create a lovely attitude in the office or the home.

Some minds like to focus on why a certain reality has or has not occurred. The many unknowns in answering the why question cause any answer to be only a guess and inaccurate. Asking why questions are a big distraction the mind learns to use to avoid moving forward. Why questions can create more stress for you.

You can be so afraid and defensive that you refuse to leave the house, refuse to drive, refuse to fly, and so on; the list is endless. The mind is powerful, scaring you into paralysis in a vain attempt to avoid the improbable and imagined outcomes. Are you a psychic? If you have the ability to create your destiny, will you create these frightening imaginations if you venture out into the world? The answer is probably not, since you are going to be focusing on being protected. You will not enjoy the outside experience if you are constantly worried. Breathing and relaxing doesn't keep you from being safe. It helps your mind to think more clearly. Look at the world and remember that you can access your defenses in the millisecond that you need them, and they will be more effective for a rested person than for a depleted stressed out human being.

Worry doesn't work. The mind is dwelling on fearful possibilities and is not the same as a mind dwelling on the solutions to problems. Does your mind have a plan of action? If your fears don't require a plan, then they may require relief in the form of stopping the thoughts, taking a deep breath, and relaxing!

Remember to always observe the mind. Your mind can be your tool instead of your boss. Observe how it keeps answering why questions without access to all the facts! Observe how your thoughts create feelings that may be unnecessary for your continued peaceful existence. Observe how your mind is motivating you, depressing you, creating anxiety for you, or promoting peace. Observe your mental talk and how it makes you feel. Notice the conclusions you draw from what you sense, and how much of the conclusion is guesswork! Observe your mind. What is your mind trying to accomplish? Is this goal the same as your stated intention about your life?

Observe your whole being when you have a problem; your mind, the thoughts, the emotions, and the physical sensations. Remember that even small problems can trigger your survival hormones like adrenaline and cortisol, which deprive your brain from oxygen and blood flow. It often begins with change, triggering your fearful defenses and then creating more thoughts and physical discomfort. Surely, if a rattlesnake or other danger is not really present, you could choose another response at any time during this experience of fear? Ask yourself, "Where is that real danger anyway?"

Go back and look and think about your list of problems! What exactly are your fears in each item on your list? Look again. How close to an imagined nightmare are these fears? What is the worst thing that could happen if the worst thought came true? What is your fear? When you dwell on fear, how do you feel, emotionally, physically, and spiritually? Fear creates discomfort in you. It is a negative experience. Your body becomes tense and often you feel spiritually vacant or abandoned.

How has dwelling on your fears improved your life or the lives of others? Have others ever told you anything about your process? Perhaps, you have been told that you worry too much, or that you need to worry more?

Maybe you don't worry too much? What do you do instead of worry? Be sure to observe how you handle your problems, and by handling, I mean this loosely. Avoidance is a way of handling fear. Lots of people drink too much alcohol every evening to escape stress, and they call it having fun. Drinking alcohol instead of worrying will work in some ways but is detrimental in others. Drinking alcohol is a form of self-medication, numbing out the uncomfortable feelings and in no way creating a solution. It is a crude way of dealing with stress, only slightly better than dwelling on worry, because in the long run, avoidance will create more stress.

Why would your mind dwell on worry? Remember, the mind is survival driven! You are given this great tool, the mind, which sorts out and categorizes all the sensory input in your environment. You are recording information and putting it in categories right from the time you enter this life. Sensory input that affects your well-being is a priority to the mind. This prioritizing of dangerous information helps to keep you alive!

As we discussed in the preceding chapter, the mind lies. The mind easily makes mistakes about the danger in the environment, because the mind can link danger with something really mundane. It could overreact to every little change, or the mind may overlook something quite dangerous because it misses the truth. Remember, the mind can be sneaky and you don't always have access to all of your motivations when the mind is directing your actions. You can easily make mental decisions based on fear and those decisions can easily create more problems.

The mind has markers or triggers about traumatic or troubling events. A trigger could be defined like the definition of a noun. It can be a person, a place, or a thing. It could be a smell or a symbolic situation. For example, you could love the smell of gasoline, which is not good for you, because your dad would let you pump gas with him, and you remember the experience as wonderful. You could be triggered because you get put on hold when you are calling someone, because, as a child, you always felt like your parents put your needs on hold.

You are said to be triggered when you have a huge emotional reaction to an event in your life, especially when you have a reaction that doesn't match the situation. That example would be when you love the smell of gasoline, but it is usually disliked and is caustic to humans. The feelings in this case are highly positive. However, the triggers that really bother everyone are the emotionally painful reactions that can occur without warning.

Please note that the mind is attempting to link your reactions to your continual survival, but that the mind is not always accurate. Keep remembering that the mind lies. Watch to see if your reaction is matching the reality of the situation. Memory is not always correct because it was based on your perception at the time, like maybe you had the perception of a three-year-old. The way to tell that you have a trigger is through the tool of observation. If you have a pleasant feeling around an unpleasant odor, then you are out of context. You don't match! If you start screaming over a small problem, then you don't match. If you feel very irritated over a small noise, then you don't match. If your actual survival is not being threatened, but you are having a survival reaction, then you don't match.

Until you are an astute observer, make sure that you feel safe first and then observe your reaction after you are safe. Sometimes, people will have an out of body experience, or a panic attack when they cannot really see a reason why they should be afraid. If these intense warning systems are going off, get to safety and trust your instincts. These reactions could be correct instincts, and instincts are often correct. You can dissect the situation from a safe distance, observing how closely your thoughts are actually matching your reality. Out of body experiences can be triggered by a near-death situation, which you are unaware of. Panic attacks can have many causes, such as a physical issue such as low blood sugar, or something like ongoing stress that you think you are handling such as an unfulfilling marriage.

It is really strange that the mind that has many triggers usually will not keep you as safe as a mind with fewer triggers. The person who has a less traumatic childhood will usually have a less traumatic adulthood with fewer triggers. The exception to this is when you have an obsessive mind. Then, your mind is stuck obsessing on many topics, which are unnecessary to survival. A person with an obsessive mind will not be as safe as one without an obsessive mind, because it is too distracted and anxious with its thinking circles to make good choices. Remember that the brain is deprived of blood flow and oxygen when you are stressed. Mentally obsessing on your problems and multiple childhood triggers will cause this deprivation.

Melanie has an obsessive mind, and really doesn't know that her obsessing is making her sick. She is tired and worn out all the time because her mind is beating her into constant perfectionist actions. Deanna, on the other hand, is not at all obsessive, but she is an addict in recovery. Deanna's mind is an escape artist and will escape over infinitely small changes in the environment. Addicts are very sensitive to change. She attends Alcoholics Anonymous meetings daily if possible, and had a very destructive lifestyle until a few years ago. She has been in recovery long enough to brave branching out into this long weekend experience. But she is nervous about this event as well. At first, she felt the strange negative energy from Melanie and it was unsettling, but now she is here for Deanna. Her attitude is summed up with her mental statement, 'I cannot let myself get sucked into her crap. I am here for me, and no one is going to ruin this experience for me. Melanie can be a cold one.' Thankfully, Melanie's energy toward Deanna shifted rather quickly, but why? Melanie relaxed and when she did, her survival defenses and need to control also relaxed somewhat. She saw her partner, Deanna, in a new light; as a child, innocent and lovable. At that point, her energy shifted and she ceased to be a threat to Deanna's mind, helping to decrease Deanna's need to escape. Deanna is a person with many triggers.

The number of triggers you have depends on how traumatic and dysfunctional your life has been. For example, if as a child you were beaten every day in a yellow room, as an adult, you may find yellow rooms unsettling or frightening. You may avoid yellow rooms. You may have consciously forgotten the color of the room, marking the beatings only with an intense dislike of yellow. The mind makes a mistake with the color yellow. Yellow is not a threat to your survival. But you can easily see that yellow could be a trigger of threat, or a marker of threat because the mind linked the beating with yellow. Everyone has triggers or markers that create defensiveness in the face of no need for defense. Avoiding yellow rooms may in fact keep you from noticing that one yellow room could be the safest room presently available. Let's say you have the choice between a yellow room or to be outside in a hurricane. If your trigger is strong enough, you will stand outside in the hurricane to avoid the scary yellow room! You can see how a traumatized person can be less safe than a person without trauma. If you were to work on this issue, understand and remember your yellow trigger, yellow might never become your favorite color. You would, however, be able to enter the yellow room to get out of the storm, and you could even laugh about the fact that yellow could be a problem. You would relax as fear left. When you relax, you exhale.

Defenses are the mind's attempt to protect you from the threatening event. Examples of defenses can be distilled into three responses called: flight, fight, or freeze. Look at various forms of these three responses. An example of flight is getting drunk! Of course, getting on an airplane and leaving town is another form of flight. The defense of fight is fairly self-explanatory. Fight can be as simple as the tone in your voice getting harsh, or as destructive as committing murder. Your body feels tight and ready for action. The action you take is violent, aggressive. Freeze is one of the more puzzling responses. Your voice doesn't work. Your legs don't move. You are frozen. This paralyzing response can be scary in itself. Sometimes, people with strong freeze responses will not stand up for themselves in various situations, and will not solve problems because their mind refuses to move in that direction. Flight, fight, and freeze are all survival defenses that help to keep you alive in danger. The definition of danger is contained uniquely in each person's mind, and as we have seen, the danger may be easily imagined.

Psychology delves into the defenses of human nature, and gives defenses names like projection, sublimation, repression, displacement, and dissociation. All of these defenses could probably be placed within the flight, fright, or freeze categories.

Dissociation, moving away from your feelings with numbness, is like a freeze mechanism that feels like you are fleeing. It is one of the choices that the mind has when the body is trapped in a perceived or real life-threatening situation. I use the word perceived because the mind can feel life-threatened even though you are not in danger. The mind creates defenses so that you can get away from pain and suffering. If there is no escape defense, the mind creates mental defenses such as dissociation. Post Traumatic Stress Disorder, PTSD, is the most commonly discussed dissociation problem, often associated with soldiers of war. You can easily dissociate over a trigger, whether remembered or not remembered, which is often accompanied by feeling crazy. Since you cannot see a reason for feeling numb and detached, you are not matching, and this can be scary.

In dissociation, the mind leaves the body and numbs out. The memory is often forgotten instantly by the mind and stored in the body. When a memory like this is remembered, it is sometimes found as a body memory, which means you have a sensation in your body, but have no knowledge of what caused it. One then tries to figure out what caused the body memory. Obviously, the mind felt so confused, afraid, and trapped, that it deserted the body! Suffice it to say for now, that having body memories means that you were once in a very painful situation in which you perceived that you had no escape.

Projection, another mental defense, is a defensive posture that anyone may use, but the problem is that some of us will use the same defense every time we feel uncomfortable. Defensiveness, as it is called, doesn't foster good relationships. With projection, you will accuse another person of doing what you are doing! This defense is a favorite defense of people with addictions. Unable to tolerate emotional pain, the projection removes the responsibility of creating pain, and instead, places the blame on another person, usually the person in pain. The addictive person flees from emotional pain by using a substance, and will also use projection as a means of removing an emotion and turning it against another. The receiver of a projection is often dumbfounded when this happens, and often attempts to correct the projector. That defensiveness further convinces the projector that the projection is accurate. Learning to speak in the language of the addict/avoider is the subject of another book!

When a person finds a substance like drugs or alcohol to help them escape, the substance is the defense. The substance will often be life saving in the beginning. Beware! A substance abuser is an escape artist, leaving so quickly that they may think they are just going to a party. What are you escaping if you crave something like ice cream, sex, spending, or you name it? Observe how much self-medicating your mind requires and you will find your stress.

We all seem to have a capacity to leave parts of ourselves behind. To make matters worse, you can be dissociating from your body, your environment, and your connection to all other humans, to God, and the rest of the universe. The mind often thinks that in its isolation, it is all that exists, an isolated ego. In this loneliness, the most important activity could be instantaneous gratification. Then, the mind can separate itself from the rest of reality in order to comfort itself. This quest for happiness of the moment is never really satisfactory because you are so much more than a brain and a body. If you remain dissociated from yourself, from your inner child, from your inner wisdom, from your connection to the rest of the universe, you are destined to be lost until you become integrated. By integration, I mean an acceptance of the whole rather than living like you are disconnected parts that have little or no interaction with one another, and in a weak or absent acknowledgment to the rest of creation.

There are many healthy alternatives for coping with problems besides our natural defenses like dissociating, escaping, and denial. These healthy integrated approaches require observation, acceptance, time, training, and practice. First, you allow time to take care of yourself. Continually observe your mind, body, and heart to accept that you don't know. The mind doesn't know. With acceptance of how you are and that you don't know, you begin to train and then practice being comfortable being out of control. You can learn to use self-hypnosis, a controlled dissociation, in order to meet and greet the many parts of your inner being. When change occurs and you feel triggered, you learn to use relaxation. You can practice alleviating your physical, and subsequently the mental stress with relaxation. When you encounter fear, you will have tools to use that can allow you to stay present in the moment. All the meditations, breathing techniques, drumming, journaling, silence, yoga, and chanting at Destiny are ways of dealing with the mind, fear, and stress. Finally, you can become more and more integrated. Integration will mean that you have a connection with a higher power, one with something greater than your mind.

To handle life, to create your destiny, to become more and more integrated, you will focus on solutions that you find in a connection with your higher power. Loving solutions automatically create a more relaxed atmosphere, both internally and externally.

Love is a solution. Applying love to every problem will create a profound healing. When you switch to love, your fear becomes energy that you can use to create, to motivate, and inspire. Love changes your energy, and in turn, it alters your reality.

Your problem list about change and fear immediately alters with help from your higher power. Think about applying loving solutions to your problem. What happens? Notice how you feel when you apply love instead of fear to the list. How are your feelings different than when you are in fear? You have the fearful feelings and sensations. Fearful feelings are described as unpleasant. The emotions associated with fear such as anger and anxiety are said to be negative emotions. The mind made monsters of your problems, like the monsters you encounter in the nightmare. They haunt your mind with negative thoughts. They take up valuable space in your daily life, and build walls around your heart. With the loving solution, fear is integrated as energy to accomplish your goals.

Think of worry as an indicator light on the dashboard of your car. Worry means you need an oil change! But instead of changing the oil, the mind gets stuck on looking at the oil light over and over and over and over. Make the plan to change the oil and then fear becomes the energy to accomplish the task. The light goes out!

Are you worrying about the safety of another person? How,

you may say, could you make a plan to release that worry, when you have no control about their safety. You are overlooking a plan! Yes, it's true you cannot keep people safe even if you could lock them in their rooms for life. But you are overlooking a plan. You are looking at that oil light over and over and over and over. You cannot control others, and continuously trying is defeat. If another complies with your control, then you have lost because the other person will resent you. I am talking about adults here. Three-year-old children still need lots of loving restrictions, just like the mind needs a higher power to give you the direction to handle your life.

If you are in denial about any part of your life, the higher power will correct your perception. In denial, you don't see what is going on right before your eyes. Observation will disintegrate denial. A fast way to get out of denial is to listen to what others are trying to tell you. Ask the people around you if they are worried about something that you are doing. You may not like the answer. What if they say they are worried about your drinking, gambling, eating, sexual choices, relationship choices, and so on? If you are turning to your higher power when you have fear, then you would not be turning to the endless other crazy self-centered solutions the mind may suggest.

Remember that worry or fear has a function, like the light on the dashboard has a function. Worry is a button in your mind that tells you that you have fear. Worry is a warning system that can remind you to talk to your higher power.

Changing the oil requires that you stop looking at the light and shift your focus to the solution. Let's say that the oil light comes on and you swear up a blue streak and grab a beer. How does that help? Or, let's say that you lose a night's sleep thinking about the light. How does that help? Sure, it sounds stupid in this example, but how many of us have responded to stress/fear in similar ways? In both cases, the excessive use of grabbing the beer or losing sleep is detrimental to your life on this planet.

You could keep asking people who tell you what you want to hear, or you could keep asking the brain that keeps creating problems for you. Or, you could ask that angel AKA, your higher power that hopefully you have, or have been pretending to notice. If you keep having the same problem and if you are having big troubles or troubles that you cannot solve, look inside and find something bigger than your fear, than your mind. Find your higher power for the best advice about how to find a loving solution for your life.

Move your consciousness to your heart to find love. At some point, you may be asking why your mind would want to create negative thoughts and feelings. The answer is that the mind works the way the mind works, and again notice that with the why question, you don't create a solution. To create a different outcome, a different way of creating, you have to look in a new direction. As you change the direction of your view either inside or outside, remember that you are looking for something unbelievable. Your higher power has that expanded view.

The unbelievable can begin with the discovery of your higher power. You are lost if you are disconnected by a know-it-all brain. Within every person is access to a higher self, a self that is more highly evolved. Inside of you is a higher self part of you that knows the right direction to advance your life toward what you could call your path or mission in life. This self is the part of you that is connected to God, your higher power, or to the energy of the whole of creation. Perhaps you are already in contact with the higher self. Remember your higher self when you are in fear. Ordinary reality, the reality you have come to accept as the only reality, can be so distracting that you may fail to notice your higher self, or maybe you quickly put it away when you do notice.

What if you have no faith in anything that you cannot sense?

What if you think all of this higher self or higher power theory sounds nice, but you just lack faith in anything but your mind? I am hoping that you have been observing your mind's activities enough at this point that you have caught it lying. And if you have caught the mind in its quandary, I would implore you to move your consciousness to your heart, to seek out a more evolved part of your nature. Believe in your own higher self first, and see if it works out for you. See if you move in a direction that you have not previously been able to find, or to trust. Or if you already have contact with a small voice inside that is your guidance, or something like your own conscience, then begin asking the question of how you can create a path that you may not believe exists.

The new direction is not the same path that you travel for your distractions, but distractions are still leading you to the path. It is one of those paradoxes that you are always moving in the right direction. You could travel next door by going around the world in the opposite direction. Remember, some paths are just shorter than others, and some are a lot less painful. Your inner guidance could speed up the process, and could decrease some of the suffering involved. For example, you could be drinking so much that you lose everything; your family, career, etc. Then you turn to God. This path is a difficult and painful path to God, but a path nevertheless.

A long time ago, I was thinking about this distraction paradox in my life and the lives of those around me. I can excel in creating lots of pain. As soon as I get myself enmeshed in all the self-created pain, I start to look for help. I decided to always keep talking to God, my own higher self, and consult wise people. I quit waiting for a crisis. What if you could accept that you could use the help of something greater than your own mind? Guess what happens? Many of the big dramas that you create will disappear. Their purpose is no longer needed. Their purpose is to get you connected.

Did all suffering cease for me? No. Since life always has change, you will always have the challenges of adjusting to change. What happened is that suffering decreased. It doesn't last as long, and I am comforted by the presence of my connection to all that is. Life is like a wave pattern that flows up and down, good and bad with times of stillness, like it is in a holding pattern. All of these movements are interacting with our intentions, and taking us to places we may love or hate, and all the states in between.

When you are talking to your higher self and to God all of the time, you will still have problems and loss, but the answers are so much faster and quicker to obtain when you have ongoing contact with something higher than your mind. You will have the comfort of peace during the downsides of life.

When you move to a higher perspective than survival, you will continue respecting your need to survive, and you will also experience peace, love, and compassion. This experience is a place of multidimensional awareness and a place of enlightenment. You will be holding many realities in your consciousness at the same time, rather than being in the firm grasp of only one ordinary reality. Integrating fear and love is not always easy. You can be tempted by your old ways, by your mind's need to feel safe and controlling. When you are integrated with your higher power, you will feel your childlike neediness and innocence being guided by an angelic light, and your fear will transform into your energy to create life.

No one really knows how much reality you can hold at one time. It appears to be unlimited. You will be quite different from the horde of humanity when you are expanding in consciousness rather than restricting consciousness. Relax. When you look out into the infinite, your initial discomfort is your own mind's current survival limitation of reality.

Finding a higher self is easy since it was never lost. The higher self is waiting for you to remember. Your higher self wants to be of service to you at all times! Remember that this part is the angelic part of you. It is as if you also have an angel on the inside of you, and it is waiting for you to be quiet long enough, still long enough, away from your mental distractions long enough to hear the wisdom inside. You can imagine this experience as having a part of you that is connected with everything else in existence, like a "collective unconscious." (Jung, 1934), which could be another way of saying God. Think of this part of you as the energy of which you are composed, and it is connected to all other energy in the universe. When you are tapped into the matrix, you have access to everything at every moment.

Please define your higher self and higher power to match your religious understanding. Do not allow your present religious belief or lack of belief to cloud your contact with an important part of yourself. You could be in fear that this contact would be evil. If the higher self gives you evil advice, then you have not made contact. You have found something else, a dark side or shadow side which certainly is in creation by humanity at all times. Denial of the dark side will not control it. The so-called dark side or shadow self is nothing more than fear. Ask someone for help in understanding anything unpleasant you find within. Denial or suppression doesn't work and in fact is a powerful creator of your destiny.

Inside of you, a higher self is awaiting your search. You have it within you to find comfort and compassion. The higher self is always watching and waiting for you to communicate. Remember, your higher self is the part of you that is in communication with all that is or your higher power.

Have you ever heard a warning, sort of like a little premonition, and then the event occurs? It sounds like your mind but in this case the little voice you hear is prophetic. It can be just a little warning. Like one time I had a one hundred-dollar bill in my hand and all of a sudden a little voice whispered to me just as I was putting it in my pocket, saying, "Don't put that in there, you will lose it." The information came very quickly, so quickly that I almost didn't notice it. I promptly ignored the voice, put the money in my pocket and left for work. Later that day, the money was gone. Was it a coincidence? You could hope so. You could think so. Or maybe it was one of those self-created prophecies, which now begins to look like the absolute truth.

What are coincidences anyway? If you are beginning to accept that your mind is contributing to the creation of your reality, then how can coincidences ever seem the same? After all, the mind is deciding about the meaning of your world as well as stimulating the release of energy directed toward your creations. You are the energetic magnet drawing events into your space and time.

Many events that you call coincidences could be messages from your own higher self. The higher self is sometimes your own personal psychic. It tells you about the future. It could be that the higher self is the part of you that puts it all together, both what you know you are sensing and what you are not aware of sensing. You already know many things about the future because if you just observe what you are thinking and observe what your life is like right now, then you can see that your future is being created by these activities. Others are creating reality also, and you are affected by your interactions with creations as well. But who will be around you. Much of who, what, where, when, and how will create your why later on. Who is deciding your life? Who is in charge of your who, what, where, when, and how?

The so-called bad things that happen to us are often events

that we don't think about. Contradictions are the number one reason that the mind decides that it is easier to opt out of life and live a life of distractions. Yes, of course, many events occur that we don't consciously create. You create your reality about what occurs. You create your direction. You create your interpretation. And yet you are part of a whole group of creators, the collective consciousness. If your higher self is plugged into the collective consciousness, then you could have some great direction for how to be in the best place at the right time. Listen to the direction. Have faith in the information offered in the direction. If the higher self says to change lanes when you are driving, you could save yourself from an accident. It has happened to many people, including me.

Mass consciousness is taking place. Everyone is thinking and creating. You do not get to control everyone, but you do get to decide your own thoughts. In being tapped into the mass consciousness, your higher self can give you information about your path through the mass of humanity. You have a path in the whole. The higher self is showing you your path. Get a new perception from your higher self. Others are creating realities and you can choose in or out! Now, escapees out there, I am not suggesting you run away unless you are in physical danger. I am talking about finding a source greater than your mind for dealing with life. Standing perfectly still, your reality will shift when you shift your focus. It is like magic. It is a miracle.

When you are integrated with your higher self, you begin to consciously realize that you can sense the energy of other humans. You are aware of the feelings of others. An infant senses the emotions of those around them. You still have this ability, but the mind may have been interfering with thoughts and reactions. Beyond sensing energy, humans also demonstrate telepathic energy sensing. If you are placing forth a load of energetic output about another person, that person can call you on the phone, even though you are on the other side of the world from each other. What kind of energy would your higher power tell you to project to others? The answer is that you would project the energy you would most like to receive, like the Golden Rule.

Pay attention to the energy of other drivers on the road, or other people in a room full of people. What are you sensing? Can you make some decisions based on this information? Yes, you can, but remain aware that the mind is constantly fabricating explanations about what you are sensing. The higher self will not make these mistakes.

You could be sensing hostility and become afraid because your mind begins its survival talk. Is the hostile person angry with you, or just hostile? You are not the cause of the emotions of others, and at most can only be the triggering force of an issue that is already firmly in place, or a survival mechanism that is embedded in all human behavior.

Fear can distract you from love, a point of disintegration, a point of losing contact with the divine. Keep remembering that the fear alone leads you away from your path, but combined with love, will take you home. With the connection with your higher self, you can ask about the direction to get through your fears, the window in a room with no exits from which you will fly. The higher self will tell you to relax and use your fear for the energy to fly. Fear may be the worst outcome that will ever happen to you.

You can get a little frustrated with the words of the higher self because sometimes it seems like the higher self and your higher power doesn't fully grasp how scary this life can be! It is because your higher self is not too concerned with fears that you can still get great advice. In fact, if you are in contact with a part of yourself that is not in fear, you will be more objective. It is not the rational mind but the elevated mind. You are looking for contact with the part of you that is already enlightened. You can talk to enlightenment before you believe that you are already enlightened. The enlightened mind is not only fearless; it is without neediness, making it a potent creator for your dreams. Fear blocks your creations.

Check out the inner and outer advice that you hear and see if that advice is based on fear or love. If inner advice is based on love, then you have contacted the higher self. It can be a real relief to know that you have a part of you that is not run by fearful adrenaline; a part that actually knows how to transform fear based responses if given half a chance to express the solution to you.

The more you consult with the higher self, the more smoothly and happily your life will go. You will put your one hundred-dollar bill in a safe place. You will make many more hundred-dollar bills that you will freely share with the world! You will still have problems, but they may not be as strong since the universe won't need a sledgehammer to get your attention. If you have an immense problem, you will have the assistance of an angel of mercy to comfort you. And when you consult the higher self for help, you will become accustomed to hearing it, listening to it, and you will learn how tell it apart from the mind.

How can you tell the difference between the higher self and the mind? Remember, first of all the higher self doesn't give fear advice although it could give you a warning. The higher self offers loving advice. If fear is the answer (remember fear includes all emotions except love) then that is your mind talking to you. If love is the answer, the higher self is giving you a message, or your mind has learned to think with love. Congratulations!

You can train the mind to consult with the higher self. Once you become accustomed to consulting the higher self, the mind may actually relax a little. It is as if the mind has been alone too long with the task of making sense of the world, and of making all the decisions. When your mind has a consultant, the higher self, you may finally begin to feel as though you are not alone.

Do you think that you need someone around to listen to all your problems? Are you afraid to be alone with your mind? Do you fear loneliness? Remember that aloneness is also an illusion. How can you really be alone when you are surrounded by billions of people? Aloneness is a mental deceit. Alone doesn't exist. You are never alone. Even if you don't include the world you cannot see, you are never alone. What you mean to say is that you feel alone. You feel disconnected to all those people around you, right? And you are disconnected to the planet in general because if you are connected, then aloneness does not exist.

Right now, I am on the computer, alone supposedly. But truthfully, I have a dog in the chair behind me. I have an aquarium full of large fish a little further behind me. I have another dog in the next room. I have the computer linked to the Internet, access to the world at a touch. I could literally be talking to another human at the click of a button. I have a grown son soundly sleeping in his room down the hall. I have a telephone and a cellular phone. I have television with real time weather, meaning that those people are talking to anyone who is watching right this moment. I live in a neighborhood of homes. My nearest neighbor doesn't work. Even if a neighbor doesn't like me very much, I could walk over, knock on the door, and make contact!

Many people in this large neighborhood are retired so they are home quite often. I am a marriage and family therapist, and many people would love it if I called them at this moment, and right at the moment, a client could be leaving a message for me. I live in Las Vegas, which contains over a million people living quite closely to one another. I could go to a casino in less than ten minutes and be in a large room with hundreds, even thousands of people.

And I could be thinking at the same time that I am alone. See how deceitful the alone story is? It is a sad story made up by a sad fear-controlled mind that is ignoring a higher self. Ask the higher self if you are alone. The higher self will probably laugh. Thankfully, the higher self has a sense of humor. If you are talking to something called the higher self, how are you alone? Is the higher self you? Are you talking to yourself? Who cares? If you have a part of yourself that can give you some loving advice when you need it, then you are not alone. You have yourself to begin with. Next, you have everyone else on the planet. Whether you want to acknowledge yourself along with everyone else on the planet is your choice. If you are alone, you are creating this reality with your mind. You are definitely not listening to your higher self because the higher self finds the concept of alone quite ridiculous.

I would tell you that if you live alone, have no family, and isolate in the alone belief, even if you can't talk to your higher self, you can cure this reality in short order. Walk outside. Say hello to everyone out there. Get a volunteer job, or get something to do that involves people. If you don't like the people you find, find different people. If you are always unhappy with people, find a therapist and get therapy. Go to church. Pray. Talk to your higher self, even if you don't believe in the higher self. Ask yourself, "What is the loving answer to my problems?" Most of us know enough about fear. You really don't need to study fear. Continually study love. You can have fear about love! You can have avoidance and distractions to love! Focus on love.

Fear is a natural defense mechanism. But fear is not the only emotion you are allowed to have. You have great supplies of love, freely supplied to you at all times. If you don't have the supplies, you have blocked the flow of love with your own mind. Unblock the flow by relaxing and expressing to your own mind that you are willing to receive love. Love flows like a river, a circular river giving back to you what you are placing forth in that river!

If you ignore your higher self and continue focusing on fear, then you will create a future just like your present; one of fear and unhappiness, a destiny of fear. Remember that your focus creates your present and future.

The higher self will assist you in refocusing quickly. Every time you find yourself in fear (remember, any emotional behavior except love is fear), ask your higher self to help you refocus. Ask for the loving solution! Ask for fear to be transformed into the energy for a loving solution! Then you will refocus on love. The more you focus on love, the more your future will be one of love.

The higher self is possibly sending you a message at this very moment. It may have been sending you many messages for a long time. Maybe your higher self bought you this book. Perhaps you have heard these messages and perhaps you have forgotten. The higher self wants to interact with you always. Listen, God is speaking through your higher self, through every drop of creation in which you swim.

The energy beneath the surface of reality appears to be connected, intelligent, and communicating with us. We cannot decipher these messages because our brains are accustomed to communicating through our five ordinary senses, and not with this infinite reality as a whole.

Meeting yourself requires that you decide who your self is! I guess this may seem like a foreign concept unless you have multiple personalities, and know that you have multiple personalities.

When you are functioning as a brain that you never observe,

running amok, the ultimate and only power in your universe, then you may wonder why your life is not turning out the way you would like it to be, because you can have one intention blocking another with these splits going on. Think, for example, that you have a love for chocolate ice cream, and an adult thought that you need to lose weight. Which part of you will win that argument, and which part of you deserves to have its way?

What happens when you try to integrate is that you may have a mental block about who and what you are. If you have problems with this exercise, it just may mean that you have an issue with some part your childhood that you need a little extra help resolving. However, I still recommend that you now begin journaling about how you feel about yourself as a child and a young adult. And remember that if you have done what is known as inner child work, and have trouble with it or feel detached from it, maybe you could begin with journaling about your higher self and higher power as you perceive it to be, or imagine it to be.

Imagine that when you integrate with your higher self you are on track for integrating with everyone and everything in the universe. INTEGRATION IS A KEY TO ENLIGHTENMENT. As long as you walk around being a separate entity, you are forgetting your connection to the infinite. Forgetting doesn't make it so. However, forgetting creates your reality of aloneness, an illusion.

When you live a life of appearances alone, then you are living a life of the walking dead. How easy it is to become a façade; walking through life with no meaning. It is called the easy path because you don't question your reality. You get up and do what you are supposed to do, and live the life of separation. The bliss of connection is lost. Being disconnected to yourself is the path of apathy. The path of apathy is seen in the dullness in the eyes of the many we see acting out addictions, or just walking around in life. With integration, you will get the sparkle back in your eyes, because your reality will be multidimensional. You will suddenly be able to experience the connections between your many experiences. Your life will become magical. Integrate with your higher self and integrate with all your experiences. Integration is a key to happiness.

Now, have you made contact with your higher self? Perhaps you have been acquainted for a long time, and perhaps you are just beginning. But what can you do to increase your ability to hear and take advantage of this guidance more fully? Be still and embrace your fear. Listen and hear the voice of God.

Speaking Your First Word – Where Would God Hide Your Power?

Let's check back in on the activities of our participants and see how they are doing with their fear, love, worry, integration, and destiny.

Right now, the participants are seated in a circle with the facilitators, and a microphone is available for the participants to speak to the group this time around. They are finished writing in their journals and had a break following the "Integrating Love and Fear" Meditation. They are cued by the seating arrangement that a shift in energy is occurring, because they have been mostly arranged in reclining positions for meditations on the floor while in the meeting room.

The facilitator explains what is happening next. "We are going to officially end our experiment with silence, and begin talking again in a minute. Before you share with the group, I would like you take a moment and think about this little story.

"It has been said that when the gods were creating humans, they knew full well that we were too immature to handle our power. With this inadequacy in mind, they decided to hide your power from you, but in a place where you could find it if you would wake up enough to really observe yourself. Once you wake up, you would easily discover this "hiding place" and be blessed with a conscious ability of that power. That hiding place is said to be in your voice box.

"If your voice is your power, then you get to decide if others are going to make you a victim. You are in the driver's seat of your perception, or at least you can get into the driver's seat. Listen very carefully to your language. Are you talking victim? Are you talking blame? Are you talking illness? Are you talking loneliness, disappointment, or fear? Talk creates. Your words are matching your perceptions. What would you say if your voice would speak of love, of solutions, the words that you are given by that angelic part of yourself that knows of God?

"With these thoughts in mind, that your voice has the power to create reality, what are the first words you will say when you can once again speak freely? What words will express through you if you are listening to your higher power? If your voice will create what you are going to become in your life, then what are the first words you will utter? We will be sharing together and start by going around the circle on my left."

The left happens to be a member of the staff, which is why that direction was chosen. He will be modeling to the group how to share for this question. Plus, he will be sharing a real issue he has been working on this weekend; a personal creation of his own destiny.

"I am ready to become the healer that I know I am," he states. Then he explains that since coming to Destiny Retreats, from the beginning he has been reluctant to actually believe he can make a difference in the world. This retreat has helped him find his own inner path, the one that he will now pursue for the rest of his life. His plan is to finish his degree and become the doctor that he always thought he would be since he was a small child, but felt too inadequate to finish.

As the microphone circulates, Janna has been thinking about this moment since the last time she attended. She didn't really like what she said the first time. 'I just blathered on about some goal I had and how much trouble I had with the silence. I feel like if my voice could create reality, I would really like to say something much grander and more important.' This time, Janna is going to make it count and to also say that she is creating a loving relationship in her life with someone. She is ready.

Melanie, on the other hand, wants to say that she is amazed and is thinking maybe she has a miracle to say, but is afraid to say it. As she takes the microphone, she breathlessly whispers, "I think I have discovered that I am pregnant. There was the child speaking to me in the breath. There is my fear of being inadequate and the inner voice telling me that this is my goal. And not the least of matters, I am sick as a dog and realize I have not noticed the absence of my period. I was thinking I had food poisoning, while my son has been talking to me in the breath. Unbelievably, here I am away from the stores where I could get pregnancy tests to confirm or deny my dream!" Melanie is so overjoyed and afraid it isn't true, but she is so sure and even sure that she is going to have that son she saw, the son she calls ... Melanie as usual is speaking multiple fearful, confusing, obsessive, and for once, exciting realities. Hopefully, she is listening to herself.

The facilitators are making mental notes to send a staff member to the store during the break to surprise Melanie with her wish of a pregnancy test.

As Deanna takes the mike, she says, "I know that I am a healer also." She is shaking and feels stupid because she is shaking. Deanna is not usually nervous about talking in front of groups, and cannot figure out why she is shaking, but she knows she has to say it. The reason for her tremors is that she is experiencing a flow of powerful energy surging through her body with recognition of her goal. She feels like she wants to be a counselor for other addicts, and start giving service to those who are in need like she has been.

Sophia just says, "Thank you for this wonderful opportunity to see my child have this experience. It was even better watching Madison than doing the retreat for me in a lot of ways, like when you go to a prom and you are so nervous and uncomfortable. Then you see your daughter go and it's all so wonderful seeing your little girl do something so grown up and magical, without all the nerves of doing it yourself. I have been touched to my soul by being here with her."

Madison is feeling a little confused about what to say, and is hoping to get an idea from what others are saying. Her mother's revelation is making her feel a little misty and uncomfortable. She doesn't always consider how much her mother really loves her because she is so busy arguing to get her way that her emotions block her affection. Madison has been having a good time experiencing the whole retreat, like a little kid following the path of a flying butterfly, an innocent. When is it her turn, she says she had fun and passes the microphone.

Susan and Darrel have taken on the look of newlyweds. They are the inspiration of love for the whole group with their eye contact, loving handholding, and good energy. Both of them share how happy they are that they are here together, and what a fantastic bonding and loving experience it has been, so much so they cannot even fully describe it. Their experience is quite enviable to some in the group.

The others share various experiences and goals, along with the other staff members who also talk about their goals in life, and why they keep doing this retreat work. "Because I think the world could have peace if everyone came to Destiny," is the way one member states it.

As the sharing comes to a close, everyone leaves the room accompanied by the thought and emotion provoking music as usual, and for the first time since arrival, you can hear the sound of voices and laughter on their way to lunch.

Chapter 10 Journal Questions

1. What do you think about and feel when you hear the word integration?
2. How do you feel about your inner child?
3. How do you feel about your inner angel/guide?
4. What are your painful limitations? (i.e. addictions; illnesses; injuries; blocks.)
5. How do you think it would feel to integrate the whole of your existence into one straight and narrow path, inclusive of all reality?
6. If your voice can create your reality, what would you be saying, and what will you quit saying?

Chapter 11 God in the Oneness

"PT: What is the gospel according to Jesus?
SM: Simply this: that the love we all long for in our innermost heart is already present. Jesus left us the essence of himself in his teachings, which are all we need to know."
　–Stephen Mitchell ("Psychology Today," Nov-Dec, 1996)

"In the space which thought creates around itself there is no love. This space divides man from man, and in it is all the becoming, the battle of life, the agony and fear. Meditation is the ending of this space, the ending of the me."
　　　　　　　　　　　　　　–Jiddu Krishnamurthy

Hiking a Vortex and Chanting the Name of God

After lunch, the group is ready for a hike up a vortex. So what are all these vortexes that one hears about in Sedona? And why do we like to be around them? These areas contain purported swirls of energy according to the legends of the area. Some believe that this energy exists, and some do not. It cannot be measured and so it is only a belief, a faith that something we cannot see or measure exists here in this red rock splendor that moves, inspires, and heals the soul.

When you come to Sedona to do healing work, the energy of the place seems to aid the intentions you set forth. The group has been setting intentions all weekend, and this energy intensity is a welcome additional aid to accomplish our goals. If you haven't visited Sedona, then you can only imagine the energy that you can feel permeating from the enormous red rock structures.

The first time I came to Sedona, I was here for another weekend retreat in 1985. We hiked up the airport vortex and meditated as a group on top of the hill. The meditation was one in which we imagined balls of color to balance the chakra centers of the body. It is a well known technique that makes you feel very relaxed, peaceful, and like you are in balance with the world. What I remember of the event was that I felt a little dizzy, and as if I could feel energy in my feet and around my head. The miracle occurred when I returned home. I am still amazed and feel perhaps that this is a natural ability I have always had but had "forgotten." Perhaps this is true of everyone on the planet. When I came home, I could "hear" my house plants for the first time in my life. Before I left, my plants never thrived. They were sickly and I had a brown thumb. After the meditation in Sedona, plants have been able to get their needs met by me, and now thrive in my house. I now and forever more have a greener thumb. That awakening of my consciousness was only the beginning of becoming a kind of full-blown Shaman now. But that experience is also the topic for another book of its own.

Back to the participants hiking up the vortex, and let's see what they are doing. First of all, they are climbing the long way around a small hill toward the top. In Sedona, the rock is passionate red stone that flakes and creates a red dust in the high desert, setting off spectacular contrast with the scruffy low green trees and shrubs. The group has been advised to be aware of signs, and to beware of snakes. It is the wilderness and still full of inhabitants that one might disturb if you are not cognizant. And aware they are. They are observing the energy they feel around their body, above them and under their feet.

As they arrive at the top of the hill and find a mound for

sitting, the facilitator begins to instruct them on a new meditation technique they have not yet heard about this weekend.

"Today, we are going to practice some chanting. We will be chanting several tones while we are here. Chanting is a way to focus the mind, and is a perfect tool for the obsessive mind because it can stop an obsession by giving the mind something to do other than torment you, or create negative realities. The chant that I love the best is Ani-hu, pronounced with a short "A", long "I" and long "U". Ah nigh Hugh would be the way it looks if spelled phonetically. Chanted, it sounds like a song with long exhales drawing out the words nigh and Hugh. Remember when you are expressing a long exhale how it lowers your blood pressure? Chanting is a long exhale and long inhale so it becomes a breathing technique as well as a mental distraction with a spiritual focus of attention.

"I learned Ani-Hu from John-Roger, founder of the Movement for Spiritual Inner Awareness, MSIA (http://www.msia.org) and have practiced it ever since. To my recollection, Ani-Hu means in empathy with God. When you practice this tone, imagine how it would feel to be in empathy with God, one with God, or one with all that is. The mind can never really completely comprehend that concept, which is the beauty of the thought. The concept can keep the mind peacefully expanding into the thought for as long as you can hold the focus. At the same time, imagine a light originating from as far out in the universe as you can imagine is flowing into the top of your head through the body, into the ground, center of the Earth and back out into the universe, as well as surrounding and protecting you. The color of the light can be anything you imagine. You might see a white light or a golden light. You could see a rainbow of colors. The light is the symbol of the energy of goodness, enlightenment, and protection that you would want to find with this peaceful chanting about oneness. The multidimensional expanded consciousness of focus, which includes the breath, the tone, the meaning, and the light, can create a vibration within you that is very relaxing as it expands your consciousness.

"The mind, when so occupied, has a harder time of wandering away but when it still manages to think its ever-busy thoughts, you can once again keep encouraging those thoughts to glide past your consciousness, like clouds drifting by. If you find that you are participating with your thoughts, then as soon as you catch yourself, bring your focus back to your breathing, body, tone, thought of God, and the light. Keep bringing your focus back over and over. Don't fight your thoughts, and don't participate with them. Don't allow your thoughts to be important, to be the driving force of your physical and emotional well being.

"Let's begin chanting this tone and then we will sit in silence for a few minutes to observe the after-effects as well."

The toning begins and echoes across the valley below, a melodious blend of various voices that creates a vibration in the air and among the group. The group becomes one with the tone.

As the toning ceases after about ten minutes, the silence is much like the release of a muscle after posing for yoga. An energy of peace releases in the air. The vibration combined with the surroundings, the breath, and the culmination of the weekend theta work and mediation produces a profound experience with nature at this point. One may even have a momentary feeling of oneness and bliss, which usually takes people much longer periods of time to achieve.

"Now, let's try one more tone, "Om", a tone that many people have heard at least in passing. Some people pronounce it "Aum." This tone is considered to be the underlying sound of the universe. In fact, some people state that they have heard this sound when their mind is quiet in deep meditation. It is reflected in the sound of the Australian didgeridoo, which when played produces the humming sound. At this retreat, we have a couple of these instruments, which are yet another way of expanding the consciousness. When you play a didgeridoo, or when you hear and feel the vibration of the instrument playing, you can expand these states of consciousness just as you might when you hear drumming. It is for this reason that some of the facilitators own drums and didgeridoos."

The group commences with the chanting of "Om", and once more sounds like a choir of angels reverberates off the walls of the red rock surrounding them like a concert hall. As they end this session of toning, the silence carries them deeply into a sound current energy relationship with the nature around them.

How on Earth would chanting aid one in creating your destiny? As you have seen, the setting of an intention is the mind deciding to create a reality. And the mind can be sneaky because you will often wonder why you attempt to create a reality and cannot seem to manage it, like when someone says they want to be in a relationship and yet have never been in a long-term committed relationship. Or like when they say they want to go to the gym, quit smoking, make more money, lose weight, and… are you getting the endless picture? This is the reason that I am saying the mind is sneaky because you are saying that you want something but not observing how you are focusing on the lack of getting this reality, rather than focusing on the solution of obtaining it. Then worse yet, the poor mind may not even know what topic it should focus on to be satisfied. Obviously, if it knew where to focus, you would already have all your dreams manifested, and you would not be setting an intention.

As you enter the point of chanting, then you are entering a new way to release your ideas about how reality needs to be manifested in your life. For example, let's say that you want a relationship. When chanting, you are becoming one with God, as you know God to be or one with all; which is sometimes manifested as a state of blissful nirvana. As you observe your thoughts floating by, and even as you find yourself participating in thoughts and then dragging your mind back to chanting, you could then notice that the mind is not creating your intention. You might also notice that your mind is rebelling against your goal, almost in war with you on a problem that is long-standing and that is why you have not created your result. If you happen to become one with all that is, and feeling totally present, you may notice that what you think you need is not actually what you need at all. You could even notice that you have everything.

Many times, when you become connected to the universe as a whole in one perfected moment of time, you will find or hear a whisper coming forth from the ethers, like a softly spoken voice that states your real intention. At that moment in time, you begin to believe that the universe wants you to be filled. You are the one with the lid on top of your box, remember? You have the key for removing the lid, and allowing in more goodness than your mind can even imagine. Thus, observing the mind, and chanting allows you to create what your mind doesn't even know to create yet. Chanting helps you hold yourself open as you tap into the realm of creativity.

As this chanting exercise draws to a close, the participants are given free time to write in their journals, explore their surroundings, or rest before dinner and the evening session.

Janna, Melanie, and Deanna have decided to go swimming and lounge in the hot tub, ready for some water relaxation now. They appear to be fast friends at this point. Sophia and Madison have overheard them, and are now discussing the same plan. Susan and Darryl are toying with the idea as well. It appears that almost everyone in the group has jelled, and they are going to be in that pool together. What happened? They have become one today! OK, not perfectly one, but they are feeling bonded to each other and are reluctant now to leave each other's company. Just two days ago, they could not wait to get to their own space away from each other, and now they cannot leave each other when given their first chance to really do so!

Later on that evening, the group meets for their first real talking dinner. Every meal they have had has been on a silence assignment until now. Even though they have not all perfectly accomplished this activity, all conversation has been minimized by the assignment. Don't think that the real goal of the silence has been to make sure everyone is not talking. As you may have noticed, people cheat and talk when they are supposed to be quiet. We have participants who can stay completely silent for the whole time, and we have participants that were so triggered by the silent assignment that we had to move them to a staff room, so that they could speak the whole time, being unable to practice silence at this retreat. Of course, that person has silence but doesn't notice because the mind talk is so loud it seems as if noise is always occurring. This would be typical of people who leave a radio or television on twenty-four hours a day, or who talk on the cell phone everywhere they go. This person cannot stand to be alone with the mind. Why? The mind is not being very nice. Chanting can actually be a replacement for negative mind talk when you catch yourself in the act. Sometimes, though, catching yourself is the hardest part. The next hardest part is to not believe the negative litany that you have been swallowing every minute of your life. When you can chant, you can place your mind into the subject of being one with God. Remember that your negative talk is not solution talk, and is often creating the opposite result of what you would like to be creating in your life.

Candle Meditations and Receiving the Gift

After dinner, the participants gather in the room for another activity. Tonight before the outside Cellular Theta Breathing, we celebrate and give the participants a surprise. No, the surprise is not in the book, because it would spoil it if you ever attend. But accompanying the surprise, we begin with a story of finding our way to Sedona the first time for Destiny.

"One day, we found a site to have this retreat so easily that it was one of those perfect miraculous coincidences, like the one you see when you participate at Destiny. We tell the stories of our coincidences along the way, like the fact that I was born in the same hospital in Billings, Montana, as Cheryl Cornelius, my business partner and co-facilitator, even though we never met until we were in graduate school in Nevada.

"It would seem like you might need at least a whole weekend or more to investigate every place to hold a retreat, and then you could make a decision between all the many places you visited. But we got an appointment at a place in the middle of nowhere, and this nowhere site turned into the perfect place. After floundering around on dirt roads, thinking we were really lost, we arrived to find nurturing people and sublime energy. As we entered as a group, they offered us a delicious cool drink and a scrumptious organic brownie. As a group, we were sold from that first moment.

"Then we went back to town and walked into a store to find a gift for our participants. The first thing we found was an item that had a sign next to it explaining its meaning. But the person who found our gift didn't see the sign first; he just liked the look of it. Then he picked up the sign to read, "Helping one to find one's destiny." The gift we give on this night is to remind everyone of their experience of destiny here."

The facilitator begins to light candles around the room, one lighting off the candle of another, to practice a fire meditation. Although we may have had a fire outside at the breath under the stars, we have not yet formally meditated on the fire itself. Human beings are composed of energy, and may have energy fields surrounding our body. Some believe that the fire cleanses your energy field just as a shower cleanses your body, and some also believe that same shower of water not only cleans your body but cleans your energy field as well (Orr). Gazing into the fire of the candle as music plays, another meditative state begins to form for our group. And once again, the group experiences another form for expanded consciousness. These states of consciousness are quick to form due to the cumulative effect of a weekend of meditation.

It is at this time at a Destiny Retreat that other people offer their gifts. Sometimes, one of the facilitators will call in the six directions and create a despacho for the group. A despacho is a give-away, a packet of symbolic items placed in a certain order, along with all the intentions of the group, to be burned at the fire. Another time, a participant initiated the whole group including all the facilitators into the first level of Reiki. Yet another time, we participated in forming an Emissary Wheel of Peace, and recited prayers for peace from twelve religions around the world. You never know what will show up, but one thing is for sure; whatever happens always seems to be just right for the group.

Stars & Fire

At the close of this meditation, our group heads out to the fire pit circle under the spiraling star galaxy, to commune with luminous beings while breathing the breath of life. Theta is deep in this peaceful natural environment, lying against the ground with only a sleeping bag between your body, and the Earth feeling like it is communing personally with you and your energy. Deeper and deeper they travel until the music ends. When the music ends, they slowly realize it is silent, and more than one person asks how long the music has been off. It seems like hours, but the music has been off for only seconds, and it triggers the mind to return.

The fire is lit. They stare into the flames and again drift into that expanded consciousness that they never really left, as if it is a permanent fixture now, because at this point it has accumulated to an almost constant theta state. With the Earth below, stars above, and the fire blazing, the end of the evening begins as each one folds their sleeping bag to return to their room for a night of rest. This time, however, they are talking softly as they wander back.

Chapter 11 Journal Questions

1. What is your relationship with God?
2. How do you experience reality as one connected whole?
3. If your lid is removed and the universe fills you, then what?
4. What is your mind saying about your intention now?
5. Imagine staring into the fire. What do you hear and see?
6. How does it feel for you when you breathe in starlight and fire energy?

Chapter 12 Breathing Heart Dance

"My heart, which is so full to overflowing, has often been solaced and refreshed by music when sick and weary."
–Martin Luther (1483 - 1546)

"Wheresoever you go, go with all your heart."
–Confucius (551 BC - 479 BC)

"Dance is the hidden language of the soul."
–Martha Graham (1894 - 1991)

Sunday

Now begins the final morning of the retreat. The participants have had their breakfast together, and are talking and visiting in anticipation of the end of the retreat. This is first real breakfast off silence together, and their last time to converse in this way over a meal. They have had an assignment to observe their relationship with eating, and the energy in the food; consciously eating throughout their time here at Destiny, but how many have remembered? Some have noticed that a small sign is on the table with an eating meditation on it, and some have not noticed. It is just one of many activities for which they have heard the suggestion to observe and become conscious, although many cannot fathom the meaning of this suggestion the first time they hear it. The act of being present with what you are doing and when you are doing it is an advanced form of meditation that only a few in the world have mastered. At Destiny, you are letting go of your beliefs of perfection. If you can stay present for even a second with your life, and away from the constant distractions, you have progressed and expanded your consciousness. From this seed you are planting, you will continue blooming as long you continue to care for your growth. You will open like an ever-expanding flower.

Heart to Heart Breathing

To facilitate more of this opening, the participants are about to experience an amazing heart expansion at the close of this retreat. Seated knee to knee with their partners, music begins to play. The facilitator instructs them to make eye contact and to begin Cellular Theta Breathing. As the participants breathe deeply, the facilitator speaks, "Look into the eyes of your partner. Breathe. You are breathing the same air. Your body takes in and gives out the air that your partner breathes in and out. We are all sharing the same breath. We are all one breath."

The music playing in the background is a song that is designed to move the emotions so that the eye contact will have a bonding experience. Whenever a newborn baby looks into their mother's eye and emotions are exchanged, a bonding experience occurs. So too, today, while breathing the deep theta breaths, exchanging air, emotion and eye contact, our participants will feel the same bonding.

"Now, place your hands on each other's hearts. Place your right hand on your partner's heart and send your loving energy from your heart through that hand into your partner's heart. Open your heart to receive that energy. The energy will flow in a circle from your heart, down your arm, into your partner's heart, into your partner's arm, into your heart, and back again. Breathe!" The facilitator keeps reminding them to breathe because they have a tendency to forget to breathe in the presence of this intense emotional openness. The body breathes shallow in the presence of fear and in the presence of this loving emotion as well! Does that mean we are all afraid of love? Maybe not, but it does mean we tend to build a little shield against feeling, even when being open would mean that love would enter.

"Open your heart, send the energy. Receive the energy and breathe!" The facilitator reminds them again and again. Just when the song ends, it begins again. "Ok. Shake out your arm and let's try it again." The song repeats one more time and this time it feels more relaxed around the room. A few tears have been falling during this activity.

Susan and Darryl remain the romantic loving couple, gazing into one another's eyes and garnering a few last sneaky sighing looks from the women in the room. Melanie is thinking how much she would like to bring Jack, just to share this experience! Janna is feeling a little melancholy about wanting to find someone, and Deanna is pointedly ignoring the whole couple closeness between man and woman, because it can create such intense negativity in her life. Intimacy is a bit scary for Deanna. She wants it and she fears it. Sophia and her daughter Madison are oblivious to the others, because they are locked into a sweet mother-daughter loving look of their own, just as wonderful in its own way.

Facilitators Heart to Heart Breathing

When the song finally draws to a close, both facilitators walk over and form the group into a standing circle surrounding the facilitators. The two of them walk over to Melanie in the circle, and place their hands simultaneously on her heart. Melanie is shocked by the energy she feels from their warm hands. 'Wow! They are almost hot, and I can feel loving warmth traveling throughout my body when they touch me. What is this about? Am I the only one they are going to do this to, and why? Oh no, they are both making total eye contact and breathing the Cellular Theta Breaths too. And that music, they are singing love to me? Why me?' Melanie's thoughts are rapid-fire millisecond quick, right before she begins to cry and melt. She feels gratitude and love. Her heart feels more open than it ever has in her life. 'Thank God Janna talked me into coming. I needed to feel this love so I would know I could love my child in such a way. Before, I might not believe it existed. Thank God she kept after me to come here, and that I came here this weekend of all weekends. She wanted me to attend the last time, but I was having nothing to do with it. Am I glad I got over my stubbornness just in the nick of time to find out I could feel love like this. Now I won't worry so much about being a good mother and well… Jack is going to have to get here too.'

Melanie looks lovingly back at the facilitators as they move to the next person in the circle, Deanna, her partner. Deanna is looking like she wants to melt into the floor. Her head is down and she looks like a little girl again. Melanie is thinking, 'How often Deanna has reminded me of a child this weekend. Oh, I have had a child for a partner. I get it. I have been able to get over my judgment because she is a child! Wow, I could do that with everyone in my life, even me!' The coincidences are just too amazing now for Melanie, as she feels like her reality has completely shifted gears into one of acceptance and forgiveness.

Deanna is feeling good but her face and body look tortured. She feels completely out of sync because she likes the attention and love, and yet her body feels like a little embarrassed kid! The facilitators are breathing deeply, looking at her but not her eyes, because they are downcast, and sending energy through her heart, which she feels like electricity. 'I cannot speak and tell them how I feel. My throat is constricting in pain, and my legs and arms are heavy immovable weights. What is wrong with me?' But then she is being hugged and the facilitators are moving on to Madison.

Madison is as bright as a freshly lit candle. She is looking right into the eyes of the facilitators and has energy beaming out, lighting up the room. She is a lighthouse, so young that she has not yet been weighed down by her issues. Being here allowed her to be open and loving, something she is losing more and more in her daily activities at school. The energy she feels from the facilitators is like the energy she herself gives off to the world right now. Her mother is watching in awe as a typical teenager is looking more like the typical angel right now, and Sophia is hoping this angelic person comes home with her!

The facilitators hug Madison and move around the circle to Sophia, who is now beaming about her daughter. As the energy flows into her heart, it suddenly dawns on her that her daughter is a natural, and that it is she who needs to thaw out. Struck by the energy flowing into her chest, she wonders why she didn't remember feeling this energy the first time she was here. 'Ah, Madison has opened my heart more this time around. I was so busy analyzing my experience the first time that I didn't feel this open. Now with my daughter here and all this love I feel for her, I am unable to be aloof this time around. Here all along, I think I am bringing her to help her open up, and she is my teacher! I should have known. I should have noticed that she has always been showing me how to be more than I ever would have been for myself. If only I could treat myself the way I want her to be treated, I would be healed.' The facilitators are gazing into Sophia's eyes now, and they can see that she is more present this time around, and feel that she is receiving their energy for the first time. Whenever a participant is closed, the energy feels as if it is backing up, like it is trying to flow back up the arm.

Next, they move to some of the staff members and when

they place their hands on the open hearts of these angelic beings, the whole room seems brighter. Tears fall and gratitude is expressed. The service these people offer is donated out of love. What happens when you are of loving service in this way is that you receive the same amount and more love back, like a love boomerang. Many of the participants in the room can feel the intensity of the staff's love when this event ramps up the feelings. The staff creates tears around the room in more than one set of eyes. Everyone except the two facilitators in the middle is holding hands in this circle.

Janna is especially moved to a level of bliss she never thought possible. Since this is the first time she has ever been to the retreat supporting another person, she is shocked by the level of emotion she is feeling. It is so much more than she ever had the first time, and her thought is to wonder how high it could actually go. 'I mean, would you just burn up like you got so close to the sun?' It is a little negative because this type of openness scares the defenses of the heart a little or a lot. However, she is not closing down, just wondering. 'I am beginning to see that the facilitators are probably experiencing a level of emotion and openness that I can only imagine.'

Susan and Darryl are the next two people with the facilitators, thanking each of them for bringing their loving relationship as an example for the rest of the group to enjoy. Some people have never witnessed a loving relationship this close before, and to see it gives the hopeless their hope back, in some measure.

Susan is also surprised that she is having so much personal growth when her only goal was for her relationship. You may realize that your own growth is always enhanced when you work on relationships. Often, that growth will be enhanced faster and more intensely than you could ever accomplish alone.

Smiling ear-to-ear is Susan's other half, Darryl. He has

never felt closer to his wife, and unbelievably, all the people here at this retreat. But even more surprising to Darryl is that he felt so close to one of the male facilitators over the weekend. It reminds him of when he was little and could still sit with his dad while they were out fishing, and in this reminiscing, his eyes water and his heart is full. Never did he expect to bond with a guy on a weekend retreat with his wife! He is wondering if the other men are feeling this kind of emotion like he is.

To answer his question, they cannot all feel it. A couple of other men here may be a little uncomfortable expressing emotion towards each other. Sometimes, it is so much easier for the men to show their emotions to their wives, girlfriends, or women in general than to other men. But here at Destiny, we have been fortunate to witness the bonding of men with men, women with women, human to human, and underneath it all, energy to energy.

Body Movement

After stopping at the heart of each person at the retreat, the facilitators join the circle as the music stops. "Now we will have body movement; first fast, and then slow." With that pronouncement, a lively African beat begins, and the facilitators begin to gyrate and shake every body part, the free form movement that helps to anchor the participants' energy and emotion into the ground. Laughing, the participants follow suit. Following that song, a slow "Amazing Grace" plays, and the group continue their free form dance, taking the shape of stretching and prayer-like poses.

Chapter 12 Journal Questions

1. What is your reaction when you feel "good" emotions like

intense love?
2. What is your mind saying when you read about these kinds of emotional reactions in others, like these participants; mother/daughter; husband/wife; avoider; wisher; etc?
3. What intentions would you like to set about love in your life?

Chapter 13 Being Peace

"Every day you may make progress. Every step may be fruitful. Yet there will stretch out before you an ever-lengthening, ever-ascending, ever-improving path. You know you will never get to the end of the journey. But this, so far from discouraging, only adds to the joy and glory of the climb."
—Sir Winston Churchill (1874 - 1965)

"Remember when life's path is steep to keep your mind even."
—Horace (65 BC - 8 BC)

"Let tears flow of their own accord: their flowing is not inconsistent with inward peace and harmony."
—Seneca (5 BC - 65 AD)

Sharing – Losing and Regaining the Path

When you finally feel free of a wall of defense around your heart, and feel that bond with the rest of the energy of which we are all one, what happens? You exhale. You relax. You find your way home, and you know peace.

As the participants finish their dance, they sit knee to knee, facing their partner. They have been through some emotional openness that maybe few will ever feel in this world. Some are feeling tired, and some are feeling warm and loving. Others are feeling like they are about to discover something they have never known before, like a flower that is now blooming, closed before.

The question they are answering, the last of the journal questions for the retreat is about how they will maintain their focus on their intention, their destiny when they return home. It is one thing to have an intention at a weekend retreat, and to have some openness, but what of your intention when you get busy with your life and fall back into your routine and patterns? How will you maintain your intention when everything about life seems to conspire to distract you from it, to even tell you that your intention is impossible?

Participants spend some time talking to their partners about their hopes, dreams, wishes, and plans. They talk about how they will maintain their focus when they return home.

Coloring

Then they are all handed a piece of white paper, along with crayons, markers, and colored pencils scattered in the middle of the floor. "Draw your destiny," a facilitator says, as if it is the simplest of requests and one you could do without effort. This last task is designed to anchor the participant into the grounded reality of life again. Although it might seem frivolous, the act of drawing on the ground like a child is symbolic of many aspects of your life. You are taking back your childlike nature, as in the meditation, "Integrating Love and Fear." You are on the ground drawing, feeling yourself in contact with the ground as you create your destiny. You are asked to symbolize your intention and put it into a real form for yourself. Make it real. And in the background, children's music is playing to accompany you on this task.

Next Step Being Peace

While you are drawing, the facilitators are talking about Being Peace, which is the next step. At Destiny, you are looking at your intention, stating it, focusing on it, manifesting it. But once you find yourself, how then will you remake you? If you are not in peace when you find you, then where are you stuck, and how can you BE peace?

And so you are arriving at the end of the retreat, and the next step for our group is the next retreat. I will not be talking that much about Being Peace because it really is another book, and the next retreat in a line-up of retreats that we offer. Briefly, the retreat involves shape-shifting with the goal of - as the title - implies Being Peace. The first time we went away to do Being Peace, we found it shocking that what we discovered was a load of conflict or war. Why did we find conflict before peace? You find this conflict because in order to be peace, one has to integrate with the other side of oneself. Being Peace is the progression past the beginning of the integration we started in Destiny.

Complete integration creates abiding compassion and peace; hence being peace is a state of consciousness that produces a state of relaxation along with an expanded vision of the world, and the underlying energy that creates all of reality.

It is easy to feel magnanimous and compassionate when everything is going your way, but when everything is going your way, then everything is not going everyone's way, is it? Some of the world is still suffering even if you are not. Some of the world is still happy when you are suffering.

Being Peace is really about maintaining your focus no matter how you feel today.

Compassion encompasses more than your little world of emotion, thought, or feelings. Compassion encompasses all of you and all of existence. Even if your world feels perfect today, you would remain aware that many in this world are suffering. When you are breathing consciously, inhaling, and exhaling with consciousness, you are promoting a state of relaxation and enlightenment. Remember that enlightenment is an expanded consciousness, an awareness of more than your senses can sense.

The expanded worldview is energy. Everything is composed of energy. This energy is existence at its essence. If you are part of a sea of energy, then what road map are you using to navigate in this sea? The mind is a limited map of the sea because it is concerned with only the little space around you. Look at your map like the one that showed the Earth as the center of the universe, or the Earth as flat. It is limited. The map to the sea of energy exists inside. However, in your daily life, you are looking out at the reality of your mass construction, maybe even giving up having a life of meaning so as to maintain a reality of the known.

In the great sea of energy, you are like a person without sight and hearing, without touch and smell and taste. You can attach to the experiences your senses of sight, sound, touch, smell, and taste of the outer world, as if you are experiencing the whole world. You may think if you cannot sense something, then it doesn't exist. You may have a very limited view of the world. Then, anything that upsets the outer view is unsettling.

With the expanded view, you have a view of everything as if you are now the sea of energy of which we are all part, instead of just a drop of water surrounded by a few other drops of water. You become connected in energy. As you look inside and begin to navigate the sea, you will not be as upset by the outer appearances of reality.

Reality is constructed by your belief system. This system can be altered at any time. Oh yes, it takes some effort to escape the beliefs that you hold so dear. It is like getting off the planet in a space ship. You need some escape velocity. The escape velocity will be derived from moving your view. Altering your view can be as simple as your next breath. Keep remembering that altering your breathing alters your consciousness.

What else could you do to increase your escape velocity? Alter your view and then hold the new focus! Take any one of your favorite beliefs and start taking some deep breaths. Begin with something simple, like bad drivers or traffic anxiety. Start breathing deeply. What is the belief? Traffic is annoying or scary with all those bad drivers. Now, while you are breathing, what is your focus? Your focus is the bad driver. Your vision is locked on the bad driver. Is the driver really driving badly? Maybe the driver is a little slow? Maybe the driver is a little undecided? Are these bad drivers? No, they are not. Chances are that most of the so-called bad drivers are just not doing what you want them to do, but in fact are driving OK. Now, look back at the bad driver. If you happen to really encounter the bad driver, swerving in and out of lanes, making dangerous movements in their cars, what do you think all the other cars are doing? They are compensating for the bad driver. Who are all the other drivers on the road? They are good drivers! Most of the cars on the road are driven by people trying to drive safely. As for all the others, the good drivers are attempting to compensate for the bad drivers!

Now, your vision has changed. You are now noticing good drivers. To hold the focus, you have to refocus on all the good drivers every time you get in the car! Once you have opened your vision to all the good drivers, you will never be able to completely ignore them again!

Now, take a really hard belief like, "My husband is selfish." Or, "My wife ignores me." Breathe and notice that your belief determines where you are looking. You are looking for actions that prove the selfishness or ignoring. Your vision is tuned to the selfish or ignoring channel. Turn the channel. What you are calling selfish or ignoring is called something else by the person who is doing it!

Take the actions one by one, and ask the person what they are doing! You may be surprised to find out that what you call selfish, the other person calls trying to be helpful, and what you call ignoring is what the other person calls doing their activities in life. Or get this, even more shocking what you call ignoring, the other person may call paying attention to you.

It is very interesting that you can define reality and then keep that definition. Can you see how hard it is to have a peaceful life with all these beliefs of your experiences?

In order to be peace, change your belief about what is happening, and focus on what you want instead of what you do not want!

Will you notice when ignoring doesn't happen? No, you will not notice this if you are only watching for ignoring. Will you notice when selfless behavior occurs? No is the answer again. When will you notice what you want instead of what you don't want?

You think that you are waiting for the other person to show you attention. You think that the other person has to change first, right? But can you see that they will never be able to show you what your mind doesn't believe? Yes, you think that someone will suddenly be able to show you something for which you lack belief!

Isn't this whole notion of finding your way by looking at the wrong maps totally ridiculous, and yet this system is how the world runs reality? You look for peace when you have war! You look for love when you have hate. You look for attention when you have loneliness. You look for selfless when you have selfish, and you blame others for your vision.

Being peace is a change of vision. It is holding the focus on peace, love, and compassion. Focus your attention and vigilantly scan your environment for the peace, love, and compassion that already exists. Beware, because if you hold a positive focus, you may be tempted by that mass-produced monster of negativity in the world that will strive to correct your view so that you may clearly see the violence, greed, and lack of the so-called real world. You may find that if you are holding a positive focus, some of the people around you will accuse you of being unrealistic. These onslaughts of realistic arguments can be so persuasive that you are swayed into dwelling on all the problems of the world. Remember that problems are not fixed by dwelling on them. In fact, focusing on seeing the world healed and finding ways to solve problems can keep you positive and create miracles that change the world.

Peace, love, and compassion already exist if you will expand your view. They exist everywhere you look, unless you are looking for war, hate, and selfishness. If you look for war, hate, and selfishness, then you will find they exist also, right beside peace, love, and compassion. Just like a child having a tantrum, if you give the tantrum lots of energy, the child will continue having the tantrums because of the attention. Withdraw your energy for war, hate, and selfishness, and focus on peace, love, and compassion. Try it for as long as you can and see what happens.

"Celebrate Me Home" - Circle

Our time here at Destiny is coming to a close. The participants and facilitators gather in a circle, hold hands and music begins to play. This time, the music is familiar. These are the songs that have bonded this group into one energy, the eye songs that create tears in their eyes, a lump in the throat, and a heart that beats a little faster. In the middle of the circle, they place all the Destiny pictures in a collective collage of representations of this weekend journey. The group collectively studies the art as they continue to make intermittent eye contact with the other group members.

"Breathe," says one of the facilitators as she takes a long Cellular Theta Breath. "Congratulations. You have now completed Destiny. Remember to be patient with those who have not been on this journey with you. Your light is very bright right now. Your loved ones have been home in their ordinary reality, and you might need to lower your bright lights when you talk to them about your weekend, lest you blind them with your enthusiasm. Remember your destiny. If you lose your way, and you fall back into your ordinary reality too, breathe and talk to your higher power. Take your time to listen to energy. Then, you will always know your way home. Thank you for being here and being willing to find your way home."

As the participants begin to hug each other and say their goodbyes, the door opens and Jack looks in to see if it he can enter. Melanie lets out a little scream and runs over to hug him. She called him the night before to give him the news right after the facilitators brought her their little pregnancy test surprise. His appearance here is a miraculous surprise for her. He just couldn't wait for her to drive home with their son, Matthew. Jack thinks that Melanie is glowing with so much love because she is pregnant but she will soon tell him that she is glowing because she is pregnant, awake and in love.

One of the facilitators looks at another as they both wipe some tears away and she laughs as she comments, "Just another boring personal growth retreat!" Simultaneously, they exhale.

Chapter 13 Journal Questions

1. What distracts you from your goals in life?
2. How will you get back on track if you lose your focus?

3. How do you feel about being peace, and how do you lose your peace of mind?
4. What is next for you?
5. What is your destiny?

Bibliography

1. Buddha – Ananda Sutta, "Buddha's Breathing Sutras" Samyutta Nikaya LIV 13.

2. Cornelieus, Cheryl & Donovan Vaughn, B. Diane. (1996) *Finding Your Way Home* [CD]. Las Vegas: Destiny Retreats.

3. Demby, Constance. *Aeterna* [CD].

4. Demby, Constance. (1986). *Novus Magnificat : Through the Stargate* [CD].

5. Emoto, Masaro. (2006). *Water Crystal Healing: Music and Images to Restore Your Well- Being.* Atria;Har/Com edition.

6. Foundation for Inner Peace. 1996. *A Course in Miracles.* New York, New York: Viking.

7. Foundation for Inner Peace. 1975. *A Course in Miracles.* Tiburon, California: Foundation for Inner Peace.

8. Gawain, Shakti. (1995). *Creative Visualization: Use the power of your imagination to create what you want in your life.*

9. Hardgrave, M. Diane. (2003-04-04). "At a Loss for Words: A Preliminary Study of Cellular Theta Breathing and its Influence on Language". Annual Conference for the Society for the Anthropology of Consciousness, AAA. Retrieved on 2007-12-12.

10. Harvey, Andrew. (1996).*Mystics.* New York: Harper Collins.

11. Hay, Louise. (1983). *Heal your Body: The mental causes for physical illness and the metaphysical way to overcome them.* Los Angeles: Hay.

12. Henley, Larry and Silbar, Jeff. (1983) *The Wind Beneath My Wings*, Words & Music.

13. Hoffman, Ronald L. (1990). *Seven Weeks to a Settled Stomach: Free yourself from digestive pain forever with the Hoffman self-help program.*

14. Jung, C.G, 1981. *The Archetypes and the Collective Unconscious (Collected Works of C.G. Jung Vol.9 Part 1) Princeton University Press; 2nd edition (August 1, 1981).*

15. Keyes Jr., Ken. (1976). *Handbook to a Higher Consciousness.* California: Living Love Center.

16. Loggins, Kenny and James, Bob. (1977) *Celebrate Me Home* [CD].

17. Orr, Leonard. (1977). *Rebirthing in the New Age.* Millbrae, Calif.: Celestial Arts.

18. Carolyn Myss. (1996). *Anatomy of the Spirit: the seven stages of power and healing.* New York: Harmony Books.

19. Perls, Frederick; Hefferline, Ralph; Goodman, Paul. (1979). *Gestalt therapy; book.*

20. Rama, Swami; Ballentine, Rudolph; Hymes, Alan. 1979. *Science of Breath a practical guide.* Honesdale, PA: The Institute.

21. Shinn, Florence. (2006 Prev. reg. 1925). *The Game of Life and How to Play It.* Santa Monica, CA: Hay House Inc.

22. Spheeris, Chris. *Mystic Traveler* [CD].

23. Websters Ninth New Collegiate Dictionary.

24. Williamson, Marianne. 1995. *Illuminata: A Return to Prayer.* New York: Riverhead Trade.

www.ingramcontent.com/pod-product-compliance
Lightning Source LLC
Chambersburg PA
CBHW020052200426
43197CB00049B/265